Michelle,

for all of the laughter, for all the wise - cracks, and more... for all of the support... I thank you! I hope you enjoy!

André B.

7.17.06

SLANTED SUBJECTS

SLANTED

SUBJECTS
ANDRÉ BYERS

inGenius
2006

INGENIUS PRESS

Copyright © 2005 by André Byers

Published by INGENIUS Press, LLC
Kansas City, Missouri

www.ingeniuspress.com

Library of Congress Cataloging-in-Publication Data
Byers, Andre A.
  Downside Up: Symbols of Protest/ by Andre Byers

ISBN 0-9772887-0-6
1. Fiction—Short Stories   2. Poetry

INGENIUS Press was founded in 2005 to twist the norm in publishing. It operates to broaden the social dialogue by presenting new topics and/or perspectives with a sense of aesthetic style.
INGENIUS Press: Broader. Smarter. Aesthetic.

Cover design by André Byers
Cover photograph by Leigh Bowland/André Byers

i dedicate my first piece of art

to *the* ARTIST –

from whose Work i gain inspiration

and produce inadequate reflections.

may every declaration that is good

be for Your Glory

and all failed utterances

showcase my injurious contempt

for my mother:
my blessing,
my gift,
my joy.

I love you

CONTENTS

SLANTED SUBJECTS

Whether it is during this lifetime or long after I've passed away, I will be regarded as one of the greatest thinkers of all time. Time and circumstance have overlooked a great number of geniuses, but I will write my name in history with my own pen.

-André Byers, Thinker Extraordinaire
Personal interview with the Author

INTRODUCTION

1

Many persons have accused Mr. André Byers of being a little "stuck" on himself despite his constant pleas to the contrary. Over time, the opinion has spread and after reading the opening quote I am certain that many more will conclude the same. I can't blame them. Brush aside the content of the quote and ask yourself, what type of man would have the vanity to interview himself, the audacity to quote himself, and then, on top of all of that, have the nerve to introduce his own book?

Well, as I try to answer these questions about the author's presumably-inflated ego, let me be clear. The author is the type of man who examined the art world and realized that almost every great painter and photographer created self-portraits. The reason, he rationalized, is that every great artist must first learn to explore his *interior* self before he can truly master exploring his *exterior* world. Also, the author is the type of man who believes that when an artist presents his true self, without façade, there lies a great opportunity to present the human condition — raw and uncensored. And, well, yea, the author is a little stuck on himself.

While interviewing him, I found that he is quite verbose. His tirades are timeless, but not in the "classical" sense of the word. I mean, they are more like eternal, without end. We discussed his desire to be regarded as one of the "greatest thinkers of all time." He explained that it was partly due to his belief that society viewed him as an icon of supernatural strength and athleticism. Please do not be confused. It took me some time to understand too, so let me explain.

To be perceived as having supernatural strength and athleticism is not intrinsically insulting. It is the unspoken belief that the author's supernatural strength comes at a cost of low intelligence that is insulting. "The black man has rarely been considered an intellectual, only a capable mule for physical labor and entertainment," Mr. Byers stammered. And he isn't the only one who thinks this way. In *Soul on Ice* (Dell Publishing, 1999), Eldridge Cleaver critically observed and discussed the black man's historical image as a "Supermasculine Menial, the personification of mindless brute force, the perfect slave."

However, as Mr. Byers continued his tirade, there was a question that begged an answer. As he described his disgust with society's perception of him being the brawn that "worked the hell out of the cotton fields of yesterday and the basketball courts of today," I couldn't help but notice that he was athletic in build but noticeably average in size.

INTERVIEWER: How does society rationalize someone of your size having supernatural strength?

AUTHOR: Well, since birth I have faced near universal expectations of being able to dance well, play sports with ease, out-measure any penis, and beat up any white boy on cue. It becomes nearly impossible for a black man to grow into his own character and create his own identity when society has already given him one — a limited, inferior one at that. But times are changing and brothers like me are determined to be viewed as the complex creatures we are and not as simple savages!

By the way, while you're writing, go ahead and mention that I *can* dance, play the hell out of sports —Whew Boy! — I can out-measure any penis, and whoop the biggest, Paul Bunyan white boy you've ever set your eyes on. Make sure you write that down. I've got an image to uphold.

INTERVIEWER: Wow. Interesting. There are contradictions on so many levels in what you just said, Mr. Byers. But…but, that really doesn't answer the question. Why would society believe that an average size black man has supernatural strength and abilities?

AUTHOR: They believe I have supernatural strength because I do, *damn it!* Did you understand that?

-Next question!

With such an easily excitable temper and contradictory remarks, I soon understood why Mr. Byers and black men in general are so misunderstood. Apparently, he grew tired of my lack of immediate understanding and I must admit my embarrassment; even after our extensive interview, I still don't understand. However, during the course of the interview and after reading this extraordinary book, I have surely learned one thing: the author is attempting to gain control of his own image, the image of the black male. This is acutely shown in the opening quote and the four main characters throughout his stories.

The opening quote, within those five lines of defiant determination, the author is demanding that the black man be seen as an intellectual. He is not spewing arrogance solely for the sake of self-glorification; he is fighting to be seen as the brain and not just the brawn. Placing a quote at the beginning of a written work is meant to give credibility to the text that follows as well as respect to the author who is quoted. So when Mr. Byers started his book by quoting *himself,* it became apparent that he planned to take all of the credit, respect, and praise he felt was due to him. Indeed, he seemed to be trying to single-handedly counter the image of the Supermasculine Menial by demanding all of the attention and praise that has been kept from the black intelligentsia since Dubois.

Also, throughout the text of this book, the reader will note that the author's major characters all have significantly different personalities and situations but similar piercing insight. Again, he seemed to be attempting to create a solid image of the black male genius. I wanted to know if this was the author's intention, to paint all of the black men as different types of intellectuals:

INTERVIEWER: So, Mr. Byers, tell me about the characters in this book.

AUTHOR: Did you read it? You know they say niggas don't read.

INTERVIEWER: I'm offended by that word.

AUTHOR: What word? "They"?

INTERVIEWER: *They?*

AUTHOR: THEY!

INTERVIEWER: What?

AUTHOR: Yea, "they" — like it identifies some large and mysterious group of raciest whites. Have you ever heard a white person say "niggas don't read"? Have you ever met someone who has heard a white person say "niggas don't read"? Nope. I didn't think so. No witnesses, but niggas believe it as surely as they believe chit'lings taste good. But you're not concerned about that, are you? Instead of being concerned about blacks' belief in the most unsubstantiated things, you're offended by a term that was probably made unpopular by liberal whites who were mad because they couldn't say it...well, mad because they couldn't say it in public. You know, they say crackas say "nigga" when we're not around.

INTERVIEWER: Ok. Ok. You've made your point. Wait a minute. What is your point? Are you implying that white people don't say the "n-word"? You don't think some whites have secretly said that blacks don't read?

AUTHOR: I'm saying, my point is, who cares. Who cares about the ramblings and actions of white people? Blacks need to stop being so preoccupied with what white people–

INTERVIEWER: But *you* brought it up.

AUTHOR: Well, anyway. I digress. Come on nigga, let's talk about the characters. First, Furious is an Ivy League intellectual whose failings in the job market have hardened his spirit. This is especially problematic because there is nothing more dangerous than an ambitious, educated black man with no opportunities. However, the true tragedy is that his anger, his dangerousness, like most black men, becomes misdirected. So instead of becoming an impetus for social change, his anger leads him to a tense situation with harmful consequences.

Now, when reading the adventures of Stevie B. Easy, some readers may find his character similar to Langston Hughes' Jesse B. Semple. Hughes' Semple constantly indulged in alcohol and women; and he was simple, sort of a layman — an everyman. But through his simple thoughts came the most thought-provoking ideas. So, as a way of paying homage to another Missouri-born author, I wanted to instill those same qualities in Stevie B. Easy. The difference between the two is Easy is much more cocky, but he is still brilliantly naïve like Semple. So then I thought, alright, where should I place such an everyman? Then it hit me. In Eden of course, where you'd find the *original* everyman. So, Easy begins as an updated Adam and ventures from there. As the story goes on, Easy, usually inebriated, points out everything from the arrogance of God to the blatant contradictions in politics.

Then there's Elwin Rodgers. He is unlike all of the other characters in the book. He is a devout Christian who is very humble and meek, and because he's so humble and meek, you won't find him giving chapter long rants like the other characters in the book. Honestly, he isn't even the main focus of the story. However, given his personality, it's interesting to see how he interacts in one of the most hostile and abrasive locations: jail. Surrounded by hardened criminals, he is similar to Jesus in the sense that it seems like he should be trampled in such a dog-eat-dog world. However, he teaches and guides them. Well, he teaches and guides them until God takes control and really reveals *the lesson.*

And then there is Kemet, and he, by far, has the most abstract rants. He is undeniably a genius. I named him Kemet to pay homage to the first philosophers – the creators of the Egyptian Mysteries. He has a small role, but you'll definitely see more of him in the future. I have a lot of philosophical matters to present with Kemet in the future and I assure you it's going to be…

Snore

AUTHOR: Hey!

INTERVIEWER: Huh? Oh. Oh, ok. You're done? Ok. I was listening…something about how they say niggas don't pay attention. I got it. I got it all written down right here. [*mumbling*] *I can't believe you called me the n-word.*

After the interview, I reflected on the author's comments and concluded that he is a very complicated and confusing individual, an enigma. He is intellectual in a sense, but he is curiously intellectual. Sometimes he's brilliant; sometimes he's a bit strange. Sometimes he dances to the beat of his own drum, and other times it seems like he's just on crack, "c-walking" to classical.

He never did admit to consciously trying to create images of brilliant black men, but I think it was accomplished. Through his stories, he has challenged the historical image of the Supermasculine Menial with positive characters, funny and lively stories, and stimulating subject matter. Subject matter that I...I must admit, is a little skewed — a little slanted. But it's that slant, from the author's curious perspective, that produces some very novel perspectives. Slanted subject matter...Slanted Subjects...

We present.

Running to the depths of my thoughts and back;
Retrack.
The back   of milk cartons:

"Have you seen me?"
The name: Truth
Last seen: Running naked in Nikes,
flowing 'fro and gold tooth
"Guess you haven't seen me!"
too many,
giving the wrong description
too many,
not even searching
worse than, t.v. raising our kids is
adults who don't read, hanky-heads trying to lead,
pseudo revolutionaries
and everyone else who don't realize
the *truth* will not be televised
the TRUTH
will not be televised

So, as I point my pen to

"pen-point" TRUE

I ask you,

"Am I wasting my time?"

because sometimes,

It feels like it…

ONE TEAR FROM GOD

For decades, I was harbored

shielded from the harmful elements of the world

for I wasn't ready for the knowledge

slowly

beginning to pierce through Your protective veil

slowly

You lifted the covering that maintained my bliss

slowly

the world began to appear

and the light of knowledge revealed

the misery. the pain. suffering.

disparity. greed.

and quickly I grew. I swelled

I Swelled to fight this terrible reality

Ballooning with increased strength, I gained Resolve.

I gained Knowledge. I gained Wisdom. Tenacity.

I grew

I ballooned. I grew

I

FELL
helplessly.
silently,
I burst below

and the world remains
a terrible sight

CALLUSED SOUL

Along the line of time
"Shine" once shown bliss, gleaming over the land
called "promised"
to dark faces with bright smiles, whiles
souls burned in church aisles

        Remember the four in Alabama!

Damn'a dream sold can be costly,
with no refunds
So today I shun the "Shine" that had once shown bliss
to the eyes of King's, that bounced off his lips
'cause now *I've* climbed to the mountaintop
and I swear 'Shine' done set
beginning to realize no matter how hard we try
KING'S DREAM WAS WET
(*echo*) *king's dream was wet king's dream was wet*

kings dream while peasants toil — fruitlessly —

still seeking redress for slavery

but 'massa' he be

still only giving us table scraps

I swear, everything I gots

is what slaves had — plus inflation

where's the liberation?

affirmative action left 90% of us

still wanting for education.

Desegregation? We thought that was the best thing

since sliced bread saw creation

But it didn't help a thing but urban sprawl, and

deforestation. Energy is wasting

trying to succeed by granting bosses' every wish

been working twice as hard as whites,

      still no pot to piss

So in the midst, of all of our marches

I'm lowering my fist

gonna pack my bags like Dubois

'cause the reality is this:

Those fighting for acceptance
will forever be discontent

Forever seek acceptance…

be forever discontent!

MELTDOWN

1

The cloudless sky offered no shade as the unrelenting sun began to turn green grass brown, brown people black, and black pavement into skillets. Mother Nature was fighting back.

One hundred years ago, in the early twentieth century, a fight between God's work and man's work engulfed the entire city. Mother Nature's icy winters and blazing summers wreaked havoc on man. But in the end, her arsenal was no match for his insulated buildings that manufactured and polluted the countryside. The beauty of nature died a terrible death and the conqueror laid out his victory in concrete slabs that covered the ground and shot high into the skies.

Today, however, Nature was having her revenge. A glimmer of her old self, she perched the sun directly above the city like a jewel on a crown. She happily scorched anyone who dared to venture outside, and it was unfortunate. It was unfortunate for the city's poor who could not afford the luxury of a car or to stay home — away from their hated jobs. Miserable, they wandered the concrete skillets. They suffered the most. They suffered the most, as usual, for the actions of the powerful. But Mother Nature was indifferent, and her anger burned on.

My God, where is a tree in this concrete jungle? If I have to walk one more block to find some shade, I'm going to be pissed. Damn capitalists! I'm sure they've depleted the ozone layer already!

Hot and frustrated by his thoughts, Furious scrunched up a grimacing look on his face that earned him his name twenty-four years ago as a baby. But as he glanced down he had to smile. He looked at the image of Huey P. Newton printed on the front of his shirt and chuckled.

I'm sure Brother Huey Newton doesn't appreciate all this sweat. Nah, then again, he gotta understand. I know the Black Panthers were hot as hell running around California in those hot ass leather jackets.

Across the street, Furious noticed a small piece of shade beneath a building's canopy. He walked to the building and even Huey Newton seemed to smile a sigh of relief as they began to catch a slight breeze of air-condition flowing from the building's entryway.

Plopping down on the steps in a great heave of relaxation, Furious slowly unfolded his newspaper and sat back. He flipped past a few sections, quickly found the unemployment section and neatly tucked it beneath his right thigh. He could not risk the chance of losing the paper's most valued treasure.

Alright, let's check out this front page. Murder — as usual. Lying politician — typical. Theft — of course. Wait a minute, a rich white man stole from poor folks! That is new. It's new that they actually arrested his ass for it.

"Hey you! Do you live in there?"

Caught off guard, Furious looked up and right into a police officer's threatening stare. He immediately knew there was a problem. Looking beyond the police car, he realized that he was no longer in his part of the neighborhood where sitting in front of buildings was commonplace. He ended up walking and searching for shade for so long that he was now in the wealthy, newly renovated part of downtown — the part of downtown gentrification built.

"What does it matter? I'm not bothering anybody."

"There is no loitering on this property by non-tenants."

"What, do I look too poor to live here?" dismissed Furious. Raising the front page of the newspaper in a stance of defiance, Furious exclaimed with sweaty palms, "Man, if you need something to do, you should try catching some of these white-collar, multi-millionaire crooks who are stealing peoples' 401k money. Instead of driving around here trying to enforce where people can and can't sit, you may actually find yourself catching some *real* crooks for a change."

The officer stepped out of his car. He was not in the mood for any back talking. As a new addition to the police force, he was dealing with enough stress within the police station and that mounting frustration was finally beginning to spill over into his interactions on the streets.

Desperate to show the wisdom of his hire, he initially tried to improve the relationship between the community and the police force, but he just couldn't seem to mend fences. The community treated him with suspicion and the officers didn't outright dismiss him but he could read their looks of disapproval. They disapproved of the community *and* him. He knew they expected him to fail. He knew that he was constantly being judged by a different standard. He knew that many of them felt that he was not hired because of his ability but because of his race. He was black. And he was tired of his ideas for improving the department go unheard, tired of trying to fit between two opposing worlds, and tired of taking the other police officers' negative attitudes without telling them where they could go and how to get there. Today was his twelfth week straight of dealing with the officers and he was in no mood to take attitude from anyone else. Plus, the white residents in the plush Fitzpatrick Condominiums had filed eighteen complaints over the past two weeks concerning "suspicious" looking individuals hanging around the premise. He knew what was going to happen. Nearing the end of his shift, he would have to respond to a call from one of the residents, return to this exact same spot, remove this guy from the steps anyway, and risk getting off work late. He figured that he might as well fix the problem before it started.

"Enough with the newspaper. What's your name?" the officer asked.

"Look. All I want to do is sit in this shade and read this paper. That's it."

With sweat still visible on his shirt, Furious was determined not to be pushed back into the sweltering heat.

"What's your name, I said?!" spat the officer.

"Furious."

"Furious, you have ten seconds to pack up your stuff and get away from here."

"Just 'get away from here,' huh? Come on now, why do you think it's ok to talk to me like that? I swear, they always find the softest niggas and put 'em behind a badge."

"Well, they're about to find me putting this nigga behind bars," the officer exclaimed as he stepped closer. "Now I'm going to tell you one more time. Get away from here."

"Is that what they teach you? They teach you to threaten and arrest black men for nothing?" asked Furious with a smirk, relishing in his ability to disturb those he felt deserved to be offended. "They brainwashed you didn't they? They told you to go arrest those dangerous niggas messing up this good, clean country, didn't they? It doesn't matter whether they're robbing liquor stores or just reading the newspaper, right? Is that why there are so many of us in jail? Come on now; let me in on the secret. Nah, a good brotha like you wouldn't be a part of that, right?"

Furious paced his words, "Nah, they   told you   you'd be helping your community by throwing away the 'bad boys,' right? Right? Give me a break!"

The officer stepped even closer with the stare of a cobra that has the purest intention to strike.

Furious did not blink. He continued. "Ask your police chief why you saturate our streets and no one else's — watching the black man's every move and throwing him in jail for the slightest infraction while rich people are behind your backs robbing businesses blind with faulty transactions. Don't you know that nearly 30 percent of all black men in this country are expected to be incarcerated, and non-violent offenders make up—"

"Don't feed me that garbage!" yelled the officer. "Let me tell you something. Yea, I'm going to educate you and then I'm going to send you home."

Furious looked disinterested.

"Everyday, I patrol these streets and answer calls from 'my people' when someone steals their property. What do I get in return? What do I get back from 'my people'? I'll tell you one thing, it ain't gratitude. What do I get, huh?! I get tired excuses from brothas like you who give me a hard time talking about 'give the black man a break; stop arresting all the brothas' — like I should just let them sell drugs on the corner. I should just let them shoot each other, right?

Get the hell outta here! I'm not a part of some hidden plot to arrest all of the black men in America. We arrest those who commit crimes. And no, the police force has not been perfect, but if you were as smart are you think you are, then you would understand why brothas like me join the force. You've heard the stories. You know that police brutality is running rampant in this country. Guess who is going to keep the white racist bigot off your ass? It won't be the other white racist bigots on the police force. It'll be the brotha. It'll be *me* saving your tail. So you and all 'my people' need to try to respect us for what we're trying to do because their Blue Code of Silence has allowed crooked cops to destroy our neighborhoods for decades and go unpunished. Any simpleton will realize that black officers are the solution to that!"

Out of the corner of his eye, the officer noticed that people were starting to stare as they slowly walked inside the newly constructed, $8.2 million structure of Fitzpatrick Condominiums. He could then sense the threatening look on his face and he realized that he was yelling at the top of his lungs.

I can't let these people see us behaving like this. Surely it's better to run this guy away than to have these rich, white people calling the police chief and complaining.

"Look, *brotha*," the officer said with a tone of sarcasm and contempt. "I have been exceptionally patient. Now get off this property!"

Furious, usually a man of sharp words and little physical action, stood up with the posture of a boxer coming out of his corner for the first round. He noticed the stares from the rich people as well, and just like the police officer, he was raised with the understanding that blacks are not supposed to "act up" in front of white people. He had long known the unspoken fact that every black person's actions represent the entire race and if you act a fool in front of white people, especially rich white people, you will always reduce the race in their eyes and surely hinder the future hire or promotion of some poor negro soul in the future. However, despite the onlookers and the circumstances, Furious decided that it was going to take the entire police force and some NATO Peace

Keepers to remove him from the front of this building. It was hot as hell for one, and it was about principle for two. Everyone deserved to be respected.

With his meanest "mug," the facial expression that he and all other little black boys grew up practicing to invoke fear in any potential foe, Furious stood ground. "I don't know if this heat fried your brain or not, but you damn sure ain't gonna step to me and talk to me like that. I ain't one of these white boys you're used to pushing around."

As more and more people began to stop and watch, the officer began to feel the heat of their stares on the back of his neck. The line was drawn. The line was crossed. Instilling fear in others was the only power Furious could ever yield in this country. But without realizing it, after twelve weeks on the police force, the officer could only yield the same power. Both men were trapped in the conflict; each one faced the loss of their only source of power. As they stared at each other with their most menacing looks, the 1.3 ounces from the metal, police badge tipped the scale in the officer's favor.

"Alright," the officer said with a voice of finality. He grabbed his handcuffs. "You want to be tough. Well, you're about to get your tough ass taken to jail. We'll see how tough you are when Big John makes you his bitch."

By this time, another squad car had pulled up and two other officers were approaching. Apparently, one of the nervous rich persons thought it best to call the police before this hooligan caused the police officer to beat him with his nightstick.

They always get tossed on someone's car and I just had my Mercedes washed! she thought.

Furious looked at the onlookers with disgust and raised his hands in a signal of surrender.

Snitches. I can't stand scary white folks! These pigs just want to show off and make an example out of me to show these people that they never have to worry about insubordinate, threatening-looking black men as long as the pigs are around. Punk police. Hell, they'll have to let me go. I haven't done anything.

Furious walked to the police car without a fight. He welcomed it. At least it had air-conditioning. However, he knew that the car wouldn't stay cool for long. It was about to get hot. The physical match that almost happened outside was about to become a verbal war inside.

2

With hopeful eyes so bright, she could have sworn that she saw a glimpse of the sun in them. Furious looked up from the caller ID with the excitement an Ivy League graduate holds when he is about to start making a six figure income.

"It's them Mama. I *told you* they would call!" he screamed. "I told you!"

His mother couldn't help but to get excited with him. She recalled him always being this way. Even as a little boy, Furious' love and energy were always contagious. Although his drooping brows and tight lips made him appear angry all the time, constant fury was the furthest from his true personality. He was peace-loving and good natured.

But times were beginning to change. After four years of college, two years of graduate work, and seven months of unemployment, his mother noticed that his good nature was beginning to peal off of him. His personality was beginning to harden.

But things were finally beginning to improve. About a week ago, after seven months of searching for a job, Furious had finally come home from a job interview with great confidence and anticipation. He made the whole house shine with joy. Prayerfully, his mother had anticipated this phone call with just as much hope as her son. She knew from experience that extremely high expectations can turn into extremely hurtful realities. She prayed every night for Furious' hopes to be realized.

"I'm sorry, but we've decided to go with another person for this position. It is in no way an indication of your capabilities and past accomplishments. We all loved your résumé and interview. We just thought it better to go in a different direction with this position."

The twinkle in Furious' eyes began to dull. No longer a glimpse of the sun, it shot down like a falling star.

Furious lowered his head and just hung up the phone.

Damn, I knew it. What does it take to get a job in this country?

"It's alright, Baby. You know they say the economy is so bad right now and–"

"I know Mama. I know."

Furious stood and turned toward the front door. With the deep love only a mother can have for her son, she was truly pained by the news more than he was. She searched for the right things to say. She searched even harder for a way to help him. But in the end, she knew there was nothing she could do. It is the black man's dilemma and the black woman, almost just as powerless, must realize that no matter how mighty her desire she cannot help. With the wisdom of an ancient sage, she realized that Furious was twenty-four years old. If he was going to develop into the man he needed to become to survive in this country, she was going to have to let him fight his own way out.

Walking away and drawing in hurricane winds, Furious let out a sigh that seemed to rumble the siding on his mother's modest, two-bedroom house rental. He contemplated doing the unthinkable.

"I'm just going to have to go to the unemployment office. Can you imagine a Princeton graduate going to the unemployment office?"

"It'll be alright Michael," his mother said, calling him by his father's name. She always called him Michael when she would catch a glance of him at a certain angle and swear that he was a spitting image of his father.

"That ain't my name!" Furious spouted as if the seriousness in his response would erase the truth. After his father left the two of them, he never favored hearing his father's name — especially if it was connected to him.

"But I'll tell you one thing," Furious muttered from his lowered head. "I should've been a boxer like him. It seems like that's the only thing I do anyway: fight. At least I would've gotten paid. I gotta fight everyday anyway…for everything…everything Mama. And I'm still losing.

-I'm still losing"

"Well Baby, all I can tell you is what I was told: never give up. The Lord will see you through."

As Furious closed the door behind himself, he heard his mother humming as she started to sweep the aged and rickety floor. The rhythm was so familiar, and as he walked for blocks the words finally hit him. He sang along:

♫I don't feel no
ways tired.
I've come too far
from where I started from.
Nobody told me
that the road would
be easy.
But I don't believe
He brought me this far
to leave me♫

3

"Alright, you can stop making an example out of me. You've shown 'massa' who's boss. We both know I didn't do anything."

"Oh, you're going to jail alright. You were soliciting in a prohibited area and you approached me in a threatening manner."

"Soliciting? My God. I was just trying to keep out of the sun. You've got to be kidding me. A threatening manner? Come on, like my threatening manner wasn't a reaction to your threatening manner? I just should've let you talk to me any kind of way, right? Well, those slave, boot-licking days are over. Well, I guess those days are over for some of us. You hanky-heads, with your little bit of power, will never respect anyone but white people."

Well, here we go again, thought the officer.

After twelve weeks of arresting self-righteous Rastas, incoherent drunks, babbling hookers, and apologetic college kids, the police officer had mastered the art of tuning out the rants of the arrested. Then he realized that this whole ordeal was going to make him stay late for work after all. He began to loathe the paperwork and tuned out Furious with an even more ferocious disregard.

"Come on," spat Furious. "You're arresting me for nothing. How can you say you're improving the police force when you're still arresting brothas for no reason?! If you'll take me to jail for nothing, I'm sure I'm not the only one. I see why there are so many black men in jail."

The officer continued to drive in a silence of contentment. Furious slid back from the officer's ear and into the faded blue leather of the squad car's back seat. The leather was so worn in some spots that the blue had started to turn grey. Furious concluded that hundreds of black bottoms, from older black men to young black girls, had caused the discoloration. As he started to look out of the window, he wondered how his mother was going to take the news. She was already working two jobs to help provide for the both of them. Although Furious worked "temp" jobs, the pay was far too infrequent and too small for him to live without her help. He knew that she did not have the money for bail. He knew that she was going to worry about her only child until she was sick. He knew that he was going to have to lie to her.

39ᵗʰ Street. 38ᵗʰ Street. Man, I can't believe this!

Looking out of the window, he felt that he needed something to keep his mind off his mother's grief before the thoughts yanked out the tears that were already beginning to swell in his eyes. Talking more to himself than the officer, he began to speak in a soft tone that slowly grew with intensity and volume.

"When will y'all token niggas understand that they only hire and promote those like themselves? They don't deal with the brothas and sistas, I mean the *real* brothas and sistas, talking about systemic changes, true meritocracy, and the empowerment of the poor.

Hell naw, they only hire and promote tokens who have already adopted the white man's definition of success and all of his convictions. Y'all are nothing more than black faces with white, oppressive mentalities. I've been telling people for years that niggas got a 'massa complex.' Forget about abolishing slavery. You all just wanted to move whites out of the way so y'all could be the new massas...join the police force so *you* can be the ones pushing niggas around.

"...thinking y'all are helping us. What you don't understand is that *you* are the ones keeping us from progressing. By legitimizing the very institutions that are destroying our communities, *you* keep us from advancing. Why am I trying to school you? You brainwashed token! Don't you know that Afghanistan farmers are growing Opium and flooding Eastern countries with heroin because that is the only way they can adequately provide for their family? Just like many brothas out here who refuse to work day-in-and-day-out and still starve, they get into the drug business to survive. But trying to stave off the flood of drugs, the American government spends millions of dollars each year to help Afghanistan farmers grow food and other legitimate crops that will reap profits for their families. Instead of harming Afghanistan's fragile economy by arresting all the farmers, our government gives these farmers incentives to contribute to the economy so they can become producers instead of menaces. But…but when it comes to us niggas, in our own damn country, their solution is to throw as many of us in jail as possible without a care about its effects on our communities. Don't you see the contradiction? All of our men are in jail. Rampant, single-income families plague our neighborhoods and keep our communities poverty-stricken, and instead of giving *us* aid and incentives to contribute to the American economy, they saturate our streets with you clowns to put us in jail faster and stiffen penalties to keep us there longer! None of them or y'all seem to know or even care that the shit ain't working…that their policies have contributed to the rapid deterioration of the black family. None of them seem to know or care that they seek to help other countries' economies and overlook a potential goldmine that could boost our own. And none of you seem to know or care that the only way these institutions will realize their inconsistencies and complete disregard for us is if we rise together to oppose them. But, you know what? We can't. We can't rise together. We can't rise together and garner enough support to demand change because as soon we rise, they fathom some pseudo-solution like hiring fucking black police officers and you niggas hop on board without realizing that you still don't control shit. They still control who is hired, fired, and promoted. They still don't change! They still destroy our communities! And we still don't progress!"

"You're blowing an awful lot of hot air back there," said the officer finally. Apparently annoyed beyond control, he could no longer ignore Furious' rants. "Why don't you let me help you? Since you seem to like hot air so much, let me offer you some more."

With an annoyed look on his face, the police officer rolled down the back windows and Furious instantly noticed the difference as the sweltering draft from outside's heat wave smashed against his face. With beads of sweat instantly popping on his forehead, Furious showed no sign of retiring. His dislike for the black cop was worsening; his thoughts of his mother's pain disappearing. The officer looked at Furious in the rearview mirror with a disarming stare only to catch a slight grin sneak across Furious' face.

"This heat doesn't matter to me nigga. I'm from a tropical people."

"You have one more time to call me nigga, you hear me?!" said the officer. "You can either shut up, or I can shut you up."

"Oh, you don't like to be called 'nigga,' huh? Well I don't like to be called a black man with a police record, but it seems like niggas just ain't getting what they want today, huh?"

"You really have a big mouth. Big John and Earl are going to love that about you. Oh yea! You are going to be the life of the party tonight."

"Whatever nigga."

13th Street.

12th Street.

Furious was now soaking wet in places he didn't even know he could sweat. He knew he was nearing the police station and anger swelled up in him as the reality of being in jail drew near. Inching up in his seat again to get closer to the officer's ear, he prepared to swing with the verbal punches that could only be matched by the quick and powerful jabs of his father's. He was about to swing with the type of jabs that once awed him as a little boy — when he thought his father was as powerful as God.

With nothing to lose, Furious vented. He released all of his frustration — all nine months of unemployment worth. He thought about his mother's pain and worry. He thought about how this jail record was going to worsen his chances at employment. He thought about how all he wanted to do was cool off and look for a job in the newspaper. He thought about how he was on his way to jail for nothing.

He clenched his teeth. He inhaled.

He screamed,

"I HATE YOU NIGGAS! You token niggas ain't shit! You're what's wrong with us! Everybody wants to know why we can't succeed. They wanna know why blacks can't seem to succeed in America despite Affirmative Action. It's because of you punk-ass, token, hanky-head niggas! People don't understand that we *all* can't progress. They don't understand that the system is stacked against us…that the system only allows a trickle of us to succeed at a time…that those of you who are promoted to powerful positions are only there because you have adopted the tendencies and dogma of our oppressors. Tokens! If you didn't have to *take* your power from your oppressor because it was *handed* to you, then you niggas should realize that you are a weak-hearted pawn that will continue the same oppressive agenda that keeps the majority of us down. You don't even have to do a self-check. Just *know* that you were promoted on the backs of the poor. And the sad part, I mean the really sad part, is that we're on the bottom looking at you token niggas and asking ourselves, 'What's wrong with us?' Can you believe it? Your success becomes the source of our self-hatred. All of our lives we've tried to understand why we were born without shit and still don't have anything. We've been trying to figure out why we struggle for crumbs while others are born with silver spoons in their mouths. We can't seem to figure it out because America continues to point at you tokens and say, 'What are you talking about? It's obvious that blacks can succeed. Look'a here at black Johnny. Or, look'a here at Asian Johnny Ping. He's so rich and successful. If he can make it, then why can't you? The problem must be with you lazy niggas.' Mind you, we are the same lazy niggas working two to three jobs just to get by. We are the same lazy niggas who have earned degrees and still can't find work. We are the same lazy niggas who built this damn country! They showoff y'all 'cribs' while the rest of us are fighting to eat. A few blacks make it to the top and they parade y'all around while all of our uncles, brothers, cousins, and fathers remain invisible in jail! It's a show, damn it. They show y'all in your high-power positions but ain't shit changed for the rest of us!"

The words leaped out of Furious like he had been birthed with frustration on his tongue. Hot and exhausted, he realized that the officer was ignoring him again.

Driving with a face of indifference, the cop blamed the babbling menace for making him work late. He held no remorse for taking him to jail. While in the backseat, having been arrested for such a petty incident, Furious held an internal and raging disgust for the token pig.

That evening, as the two black men's destinies collided, they raged at each other in the precinct like eternal enemies. However, neither would see past their anger and understand the truest of their reality. Neither would step back and see the bigger picture. Although they hated *each other* for their circumstances, all of their choices that day were influenced, altered and dictated by the failures of one thing: black integration into mainstream America.

Their true source of pain was never considered, never fought.

METERS OF FRUSTRATION

REWIND

I

Like a broken record skipping

on the worst part

of the worst song

My life remains

like the vinyl–

Black and Broken.

II

Like a sentence

    fragmented

incomplete and

     incomprehensible

   "Damn is shit this!"

<u>even expletives don't sooth!</u>

for the cracked record won't break

won't move forward.

It just plays

the constant tale of disappointment,

poverty, pain

Then it rewinds

      and Plays again

       and Rewinds

        and…

I

Like a broken record skipping

on the worst part

of the worst song

My life remains

like the vinyl…

P L A Y I N G SEEK

Unmelodic melodies plucked on heart strings
offbeat and out of tune

playing frantically
like kids before the street lights come on.

knowing the sun's setting and
the good times are about to end

"Let's play Hide-and-Go-get-it one more time"
Caress and Grind
Hips bounce natural rhythm outside mine

well they used to

but we lost that rhythm

that beautiful rhythm played by hearts in tune

We lost   it
We   lost
We
are no more.

and You
I lost
under darkening skies. playing.

playing.

But I giggle no more because I only want you
and no matter how much I run around
searching
          I only find
easy-to-find, easy girls
under bright street lights
waiting for me. under glowing street lights.
damn.
the street lights are on.

I hear my Mama calling. pulling us apart

I hear our hearts' song playing off-key.
hurting my ears

and my heart sighs.

      knowing the feeling

HOT WHISKY IN A MAYO GLASS

As I sit in my zero-bedroom apartment amongst a haze of cigar smoke and deafening Bob Marley, I watch cherry-brown swirl around in my cleaned-out mayonnaise turned whisky glass. The spirits entice me, so I bellow at the top of my lungs, ♫ "My feet is my only carriage. So I've got to push on through!" ♫

Acoustic snares bounce off crusty-brick walls like wrecking balls as I passionately sing off-key, Jamaican accented bars, ♫ "Everything's gonna be alright. Ha! Everything's gonna be alright!" ♫

Everything's gonna be alright…right? *Sip* Sounds visceral…like, " Everything comes to light. So I've been told…must be why the liquor store is always the brightest shop on the block. Like all of Las Vegas packed within 35 square feet — welcoming all passers-by with its all-glass front, all flashy bottles, all neon lights, all big breasts on poster board holding big bottles of drinks I've never seen women drink. *Sip*

But I drink. Liquor stores number like piss-filled corners on my block, like cracks in the street, like unfilled potholes making raggedy cars raggedier. And it shines. The light shines on all the dark faces standing outside saying much but not holding a conversation, moving but not going anywhere, escaping but never leaving. So they stand there, loitering, like permanent fixtures on the sidewalk, like ghosts unseen by most of you who walk by avoiding eye contact; like people, our people, overlooked and ignored.

*Puff**Puff*

I blow smoke-loops now. It took some practice, but now I blow smoke-loops like my uncle used to do before he passed away from lung cancer. He smoked cigarettes; I smoke cigars. Ivy League sophistication put me in a different social class but he was obviously the wiser. *Sip*

With joy on my face and naps on my head, I used to sit with my uncle on the massive concrete slab we called a front porch — painted over for the third time. This time, it was teal-blue. He'd drink V.O. and blow smoke loops that fascinated me — large, murky circles. So I stuck out my tiny hand one day and grabbed it; stood up and placed it over his head as a halo because no matter what side of the law my uncle lived, he was always an angel to me. And I love 'im.

And…and that ain't just the alcohol making me emotional. Ain't nothing like hot whisky in a mayonnaise jar — keeps you grounded *Puff* Bad habits from demonized segments of society are usually just attempts to find happiness in the bad circumstances handed to them from a demonized society…bad circumstances and bad habits…our family inheritance…passed down from generation to generation…

Hiccup

…things getting a little blurry the more I drink the less critical the analysis but the more…more happier the moment. ♫ "Everything's gonna be alright. Ha!" ♫

I've seen the light. I said I'VE SEEN THE LIGHT!...got a brown paper-bag special while I was there too ♫"Everything's gonna be alright. Ha!" ♫

Hiccup Wait a minute. Waita minute! Gimme a minute. Let me have onemore sip and thenI'm going totell yall about…*Pass out*

EASY RUNNING THANGS

1

Scattered clothes across the hardwood floor topple each other like a million pieces to a jigsaw puzzle. They circle a beautiful oak bed with a rich, white comforter and towering oak columns. A loud snore pushes through the air disturbing the otherwise tranquil aroma of Cuban cigars and exotic aftershave that speak of a night filled with expensive joy.

In a slumber that only cognac can produce, Stevie B. Easy lies beneath his perfectly-made bed and its three plush, decorative pillows with images of Dolomite, The Mack, and Iceberg Slim imprinted on the front. Mr. Easy snores on the floor. His body, slender, tall and still fully clothed, is sprawled across two piles of clothes he had thrown around earlier that evening.

At that time, he was performing his best work: getting dressed. Putting together the perfect combination of alligator shoes, matching belt, slacks, designer underwear, big-collared shirt, gold chains, and colored mink was made into an art form when Easy took it to task. Tonight, it was the tricky combination of sleek and fashionable yet casual and lazy. The contradiction had taken an hour to assemble and press. But now, it lay wrapped around his body wrinkled and bunched together like the tube sock he usually placed in the crouch of his pants.

In a deep, REM sleep, his eyelids make a futile attempt to cover his wandering eyes. Darting back and forth as if he was watching an intense tennis match, Easy dreams…

dreams…   dream…   drea…

"Hey Baby! Dig it. I'm just walking around
to remind y'all, that I am *Man*. Understand?
As a matter of fact, I am
the Man.
You better recognize! "

With that said, Easy turned away from the dismayed animals with his head pointed toward the sky and walked off with a slight limp — a limp that was as cool as autumn's breeze. His left leg stayed straight and stiff while the right leg dipped just enough to add a bounce that complimented the motion of his arms that swung like the wind.

And he walked on.

Again, with his eyes closed and his nose high, Easy strutted past a few more indiscriminate animals with a swagger of self-importance. He almost failed to notice their presence. Had it not been for their grumbling sound of disapproval, he would have certainly passed them without greeting them in the proper manner.

Without affording them the courtesy of opening his eyes, Easy stiffened his neck even more and raised his head even higher. So melodic was his speech that he seemed to speak in poetic bars.

"As you all know, I was

created in God's image. Can you dig it?

So you know the game,

He chose me. I'm y'alls Master.

And I don't want to

have to

hurt my hand, so

behave and be cool.

So I won't have to…"

S   M   A   C   K!

Easy hits the ground so hard that he rolls somewhere between nine and twelve feet (he couldn't really tell because his eyes were closed). After shaking off the initial shock, he opens his eyes and stares up into a pair of huge, cloudy-grey looking eyes. Refusing to show the fear ballooning inside, he slowly sits up and gnarls at the creature he named "Grizzly Bear" a few days prior. The bear looked unfazed.

"You know what?" Easy stammers, his melody apparently knocked off base as angry utterances fall out of his mouth without pause. "I'm sick of you alls insubordination Don't take my kindness for weakness I run this here Garden I'm the ruler of Eden Don't make me... Boy you don't wanna see me get angry...it'll be...[*inaudible*]"

Standing to his feet, Easy realizes that none of them can hear his threats under the deafening laughter coming from all of the circling animals. They all watch and roll on the ground with hysterical laughter. Upset, Easy begins to walk away with a stooped head until anger boils up inside and consumes him. His anger grows. It swells until he becomes livid and looks around to see who should feel his wrath. Glancing around, he looks at the gorilla, the bear, the lion...ah, hah. He turns around and punches a squirrel right between the eyes.

"Shut up laughing. I'm the man!"

With that said, he turns back around and continues to walk away from the ridiculously loud laughter. Taunts pierce his back like a thousand pebbles hurled at him at once, and he runs. He runs fast and hard. He runs to tell God.

"God, I was–"

"I already know, Easy. I see everything."

"Oh yea, I forgot. So then you know how ungrateful these animals have been. You put me in charge. I run the Garden. But I can't do my job right when they're bigger and stronger than me. I just don't understand why you didn't make *me* the strongest. If you ask me, that would've made more sense."

Sitting beneath a massive oak tree beneath a massive sun, God pauses. Playing Spades with the other gods on a thin, foldable card-table, "I AM" peeks over a perfect hand of thirteen "big" Jokers and shoots a deathly glance of disapproval. The look smacks Easy in the face and he just shrugs his shoulders with a look of devilish innocence. With the undying courage that is only found in persons still traumatized by great humiliation, he continues to push.

"I know it's the seventh day and you're resting and everything, but I was just thinking, how about making some more of me? I mean, I could really use some more Stevie B. Easys around here to help me muscle around the bears and lions and stuff. I mean, for real, they're starting to get out of hand. They obviously don't know their place, and I've got to show them who's boss. Ya know? Show 'em I'm the *man*."

"Easy, you're so myopic."

"Thank you. You're so flattering."

God's head drops on the card table, shaking from side to side. The frail legs of the table shudder under the weight, and the other gods giggle behind their cards, finding pleasure outside the card game they always lose.

Sigh

"First of all, being myopic is not a good thing. Why do you pretend to know things when you don't understand? All you have to do is ask me and if I deem it necessary, I will tell you. You've only been in existence for a few days and you already think you know it all.

"Easy, let me tell you something. Contrary to what you believe, you don't know much of anything. I only gave you a pebble-size amount of knowledge, and I gave you that much so you could tend to the Garden. And you have the nerve to be egotistical. Ok. I have a new rule: don't ever eat from the tree of knowledge.

You don't know what to do with the amount you have."

Hearing God's rebuke, Easy slowly hangs his head forward. He was not in the mood for God's babbling and his frustration was beginning to show on his face. He had to hide it. He was tired of being laughed at. The animals laughed at him, the gods laughed at him, and now, on top of all of that, "I AM" was lecturing him — as usual.

"Listen, I didn't make you so you could control the world. I want you to *enjoy* everything I have made — not fight it and try to keep it under submission. You're going to have to learn to stop being so egotistical and controlling. It's evil."

Evil? Being egotistical is evil? Then God has to be the most evil out of all of us! I should've known "I AM" wouldn't understand. No one ever contests God's authority...and I'm the egotistical one? Everyday we praise God. Everyday we do what God tells us to do. What a hypocrite. God is the controlling one. God has the ego problem, not me. "Praise God. Give God the glory. Do what God

says." Give me a break. God is arrogant! I ain't that
bad.

Easy raised his head and looked into the faces
of the other gods with hopes that one of them would
speak up and give voice to his thoughts. One by one,
he read their facial expressions and one by one, with
great disappointment, he realized that none of them
would help him. Now he was disgusted and frustrated.
As he turned away to leave, God, with a huge grin,
threw out another Joker and took another "book."

"What? You don't think I can hear your
thoughts?"

Shocked, Easy turned to face the group.

God stood as tall as the towering oak tree and
slammed the last Joker on the table. *BAM!* Another
perfect game. The other gods threw their cards on the
table, gave one another a look of indifference and
joined the chorus of applause and cheers from the
surrounding onlookers. Slowly, with praise on their
tongues, they all departed.

"So you think I'm egotistical, huh? Alright
Easy. You think that you can take care of the world

without me telling you what to do, huh? I was only trying to protect you from yourself, but we'll see who's egotistical."

LET THERE BE FREE-WILL

"Now. There you go. Now you can listen to me or not, and you can run the world as you see fit. We will see how you conduct yourself."

God steps to depart, but turns around at the last minute. "One more thing, foreseeing the problems you will create, I have enough grace to start you on the right track. I am going to grant you your wish by creating a mate for you. It is not good for man to live alone. Otherwise, the animals will surely kill your fool self. You need someone to balance and complete you, someone to balance your arrogance and testosterone. So I am going to put you to sleep and use one of your ribs to make your partner. That way, you both will be of the same flesh — one and equal."

Easy's eyes lit up as bright as the sun. With a look of pure joy, he stammers, "Dynamite!   That's what I'm talking about. The world is mine baby! God! Hey, can you make him bigger than the bears though? We've got to stay on top. You know what I mean? We're going to run this thang though! I'm telling you!"

"As a matter of fact," the Lord said sternly, "I am going to make *her* smaller than you."

"Smaller than me? Smaller than *me*?! What? Then what help will she be to me? I can't reign over the world with pure dominance with someone smaller than me. What are you thinking?!"

"Actually, genius, if I made someone bigger than you, what would keep her from dominating *you*?"

"You know what? That's alright. I'll be alright, Lord. Just forget I even came over. Free-will will do just fine."

Turning around, Easy strolls away with his time-setting limp, mumbling under his breath, "I don't know what God's talking about I'm 'bout to go do some serious weight training Now that I have free-will I don't need no mate no nothing I'll show these animals They don't know me I keeps a razor blade

under my tongue What's my name?!   Mr. E-A-S-Y
They just don't know..."

S   M   A   C   K   !

2

Feeling woozy and out of place, Easy slowly opens his eyes with a throbbing headache.

"My God," he asked, "will women always give me headaches?"

Deep inside, he heard a voice: "Yep."

Beneath the glory of the beautiful blue sky, Easy begins to sit up until a tingle pinches his left side. He cocks his head to the left like a curious dog and tries to examine his side but his head shoots back up as his throbbing headache doubles.

Suddenly, a voice spoke into his ears — gentle like the breeze, yet strong like the roaring Gihon River. "Don't lean over. I know you feel a little strange on your left side. God made me from one of your ribs."

Easy quickly turned to identify the voice and gasped at the sight. She was more beautiful than any of God's other creations. She was more beautiful than the midnight moon. She was more beautiful than flowers in full bloom blowing in the wind…the wind. The wind. Easy actually took in so much wind from his gasp of shock that he began to choke. Instinctively, as if she was made to care for him, the woman ran to him, raised his arm and patted his back.

Finally, relieved and relaxed, Easy looked into eyes that seemed to pour over his soul. He loved her with every ounce of his being and felt like he had never felt before. He felt whole. He felt complete.

In the corner of his eyes, he caught a glimpse of God approaching.

"Lord. My Lord! You've outdone yourself this time, Daddy. Seriously, I'm speechless! I love everything about her."

Gently touching the nap of her neck, Easy fell into her eyes. So soft was her beautiful brown skin that he forgot God was there as he ran his thumb across her beautiful, full lips.

"She's so warm and tender," he whispered to God, to himself.

The two humans stared into each other's eyes as though watching their own souls run wild, with joy, behind each other's irises.

"Ahem" disrupted the Lord.

"Oh, I'm sorry," said Easy with a grin, still staring into the face of God's greatest work. "I don't know what you put inside of her, but I surely won't mind sharing Eden's treasure with her. I actually feel like I *want* to give her the world."

"Exactly," said the Lord with a knowing look of confidence. "You are already beginning to release some of your selfishness."

"Thank you Lord!" replied Easy with a pause. "But now that I think about it..."

With a devilish grin, he glanced at God.

"Lord, before you go, there's something on my mind. I hope you don't mind, but I have to ask. Well, it's more like a request."

Looking at the beautiful woman and then turning to God....

Looking back at the woman and then turning back to God….

He smiled.

"I was just wondering..."

"Yes Easy?"

"Ughmm. Well. I was just wondering…"

Easy clears his throat, gains his composure and confidence.

"Go ahead Stevie."

"Can I have two or three more women?"

As soon as it came out of his mouth, he dropped his head, anticipating a day-long lecture about his greed. But when he looked up, Easy was surprised to see a smirk on God's face. Easy smiled back with great eagerness. He would get his request — so he thought. Elated, smiling from ear to ear, he turned back around to look into the eyes of his beautiful mate. But instead of the loving vision he remembered, he found the source of God's grin. As he looked into those same eyes that once poured over him, he no longer saw love and affection. He saw sternness. He saw a level of vindictiveness that was unparalleled —

not even the scorn in the grizzly bear's eyes could compare.

"My dear

sweet, beautiful and

gentle woman, I didn't mean..."

S   M   A   C   K   !

KALEIDOSCOPE OF LOVE

HEAVEN SCENT

The scent of attraction
sings harmoniously across
      fields of clouds
        higher
  me
taking
where Angels blush
at my nakedness. bearing my soul
to love/to you

KILLING IT

Bouncing off soft walls. LOUDLY
                    gently
echoes carry your scent
of pressed roses. dipped in oil.
With perspiration dripping
burning holes below. Like
Lava love
pouring down the wall and
                    climbing

                    climbing
climbing slowly to climax, and
smearing, passion-filled profanity
against the soft air
'til your bouncing body shudders
your shuddering body
tightens; and your tightened body
lays still
in my arms. limp. panting.

Clinging to each other, tight
are every muscle on my body
holding you up/close/over my Talent
The muscles scream. they all scream
in the deep silence of heavy breathing
"Damn! Now THAT'S how you kill it!"

L O V E

"Dré," they say, "Do you even know Love? 'cuz
you're always so angry. Maybe,
you should try to Love more." Well, excuse me for
just a moment while I tell you about Love.
'cuz y'all the ones who are lost,
wit' the notion glossed
over and down your throat it was shoved
"Do I even know Love?"
Please! While war, destruction, and greed proceed
to run amuck, I'm stuck. 'cuz
Momma always said never answer a question wit' a
question but,
"What the hell y'all talking about?!"
I see Love all the time.
It ain't blind – nor am I.
avoiding each other's path, we try. 'cuz
I don't like Love
and Love, sho' don't like me
I see it slither in the heart of mankind discreetly
overwhelms the thief who then beats

a lil' ol' lady for her purse — Love hurts. remember?

So even December, cold can't hold

streetwalkers' legs together.

'cause they Love money and men Love puss-

Thee

Indians and Pakistanis

Love Kashmir and smear

border lines with bloody crossfire, while the US hire

troops who Love their country.

And as they die for our Love for oil, I boil 'cause

after their funerals, gas is still high as hell!

Can I tell   you   about this beast called Love?

How it's all the Record Industry is made of?

where they boast about smacking niggas and

smacking tail.

In reality, misguiding youth, just to live well

through the sale of their records, and

selling-out my culture, their poster

grace the walls of impressionable kids

growing up without a dream — already enslaved to his

gluttonous nightmare. "And the winner is…

Sex, Drugs, & Guns for the album of the year award."

Drunk, accepting, "I wanna thank the Lawd!"

Sigh

Yea. I *guess* you Love God

and at the same time

Love greed. Love lust. Love drugs.

Love cars. Love pimps. Love thugs. High above,

I throw my hands 'cuz

now that I've shown you — you can have the garbage.

I'm sick of this dark, deceitful, treacherous leech

we call Love

PO' FOLKS FOR STATUS QUO
(Easy Running Thangs Pt.2)

1

Lodged in that awful place that is wedged between a hangover and still being intoxicated, Stevie B. Easy jumps up from his bedroom floor and caresses his face. He tries to rub the pain away from a stinging smack that never happened. Trying, unsuccessfully, to maintain his balance, Easy watches the wobble in his legs rise up his spine until it hits his head like a diesel. He was officially hung-over. As his head began to throb uncontrollably, he fell face-first on his bed like a rock and let out a great moan into his fluffy, decorative pillows.

Almost instantly, he flips over on his back as if possessed by demons. With a crazed look on his face and dilated eyes, he appears as though he has overdosed on drugs.

Is that MY breath smelling like that?!

Being careful not to breathe with his mouth open, Easy begins the routine of the "hung-over." There is always the first question that beckons an immediate answer; however, despite the great need to know, the mind only produces more and more questions.

What time is it?

Aghhh, how did I end up on the floor?

Where was I last night?

What was that dream about?

How did I get home?

Oh, well.

I wonder if I can get back to sleep...

Why is it so bright in here?!

Easy rolls over into a position of pure awkwardness and comfort. It is a physical feat that turns half of his body away from the light coming in from the window but keeps the remainder in its initial place (fully rolling over would have used too much energy).

He snores again.

Suddenly, like the horn of a cruise ship, a blaring sound startles him to the point that he pops up like a jack-in-the-box. It was his cell phone.

"Yo," he crackles.

"Mr. Easy, you sound terrible. Are you alright?"

"Me? Ughh, yea. Who dis? If this is Charlene, girl, I told you that I sent that child support check three days ago. If it ain't there, then you need to talk to your mailman. I ain't gonna keep telling you–"

"Mr. Easy. Mr. Easy," the delicate voice stammers on the other end. "No, no, it's me, Bonny. I just wanted to call, check on you and make sure you were getting ready for the four o'clock fundraiser. Will you be able to make it? You had a long night last night."

Rubbing his temple as though it would help his memory, "Ughh, this is for that woman's league, ain't it? We expect big bucks, right?"

"Yes sir," his assistant politely replies to the silence that followed.

Easy pauses and weighs his options.

"Are the chicks cute?"

"Sir?"

"Never mind. You wouldn't know. You still think a flat booty is a good thing. Listen, I'll go. You never know where a cutie may pop up."

Silence disrupts the conversation again. This time it was Bonny. She was reluctant to proceed because, as an assistant, she felt that she should take orders and not give them. She *is* just a summer intern. But after last night, it had become apparent that something had to be done.

"Sir, this time, you may want to be a little more cautious with your delivery. I don't think your message settled well with the audience last night."

"No? Well, who cares? I'm going back to sleep. Call me back in about nine minutes."

"You don't remember what happened last night, do you?" Bonny presses.

"Nope. But I tell you one thing, this plush bed I bought with last week's campaign money is comfortable as hell. I'm obviously not used to having it though. I woke up on the floor again."

Bonny was shocked. This was just the type of carelessness that greatly concerned her. Everyday, Mr. Easy never ceased to amaze her with his total and complete disregard for the rules of campaigning.

"Sir! Campaign money is not supposed to be used for your own personal expenditures. It is illegal and could very well jeopardize this campaign. We are supposed to fight for the poor and middle-class, not steal from them!"

She was passionate in her response but her concern would be futile.

"Now listen, Bonny. I had to buy the bed. I couldn't take the risk of people finding out that their Mayoral Candidate didn't have a plush bed, you know? I've got to play by the rules. You know the rules, don't you? Politics is just like pimping. If poor and middle-class people don't think you're better than them, then everything goes crazy."

"What do you mean?!" asked Bonny. "That doesn't make any sense. Why wouldn't someone who is poor be the poor's best candidate — their best *representative*?"

"Girl. It ain't about representing them. I spend all our campaign money on clothes, minks, shoes and good alcohol 'cause I gots to look good. I've got to seem better than them, you know? I gotta seem like I can take care of them, like I know what's best for 'em. Haven't you seen *The Mack* before? It's the same thing. Whether it's better education, more money, better looking, or a better bed, you've got to seem better than them to make them feel comfortable with you running thangs. You understand? That's the only way to success. Watch and learn Bonny. Watch and learn. What time is it anyway?"

"It's almost two o'clock."

"Well call me back in about nine minutes."

"Yes sir, but before you go, I think you may want to revise your–"

"Bonny! Girl! Just tell me. Just tell me then. What happened last night?"

Finally, the opportunity presented itself. She knew that she had to be careful. She needed this internship to complete the last of her graduation requirements, and she risked remaining in school an extra semester if Mr. Easy fired her. However, she knew that the risk had to be taken. After last night's event, for the first time in her sheltered life, she feared for her physical safety. If this campaign was going to continue, Mr. Easy's speech had to change. So, with God-given strength and a great hope that Easy would change his message, Bonny flipped a tiny tape-recorder in her hand and prepared to play it.

"Ok sir, because you're always drunk at the events, I took the liberty of recording last night's event so you could get the full effect. I'll play it through the phone."

2

Crackle
Crackle
Crackle

[*the tape begins to play in a low, somewhat distorted, but clear volume. Easy's voice becomes distinguishable. He speaks with a drunken drag.*]

"Yeeaaaa.   Thank y'all for having me. *Belch*   First, I'd like to thank you for the decent booze.   You know people just don't do open bar like they used to.   Let me tell you…   Oh.   Let me introduce myself.   My name is Stevie B. Easy and I am the founder and 2008 mayoral candidate for my new political party, Po' Folks for Status Quo.   That's right, Po' Folks for Status Quo.   Ain't you tired of donating to organizations that call themselves something like 'Citizens for Change' or 'Center for Progress' or something like that when nothing ever changes? I mean, ask yourself, have you *really* seen any progress? You done donated countless dollars and time, and has anything changed? Are the downtrodden still downtrodden? Let me give you a statistical fact: the rich are richer and the poor are poorer. The gap has widened. And I hate to be the one to tell you, but all these years you've been duped. That's right, duped!

"But not any longer! You don't have to be bamboozled any more *Belch* because I...I bring to yous people Po' Folks for Status Quo. That's right, say it with me, 'Po' Folks for Status Quo.' You gotta make it rhyme. Say Po' — not poor. Brothas and sistas, if you're sitting next to one of the uppity, rich white folks, help 'em out, will you? You all know how to say Po'. Hell, that's most of you anyway. Po' Folks for Status Quo. Yep. This year we're doing something that has never been done in politics before..."

"Keeping It Real!" came the shouted response from Easy's staff workers who sat near the front.

"That's right," Easy continues as he fingers the event coordinator over towards him. "Hey, can you bring me something to drink? Oh. Oh, it's already up here? Well, I don't see it. Oh. Oh, ok. Here it is. I see it. As a matter of fact, we just finished an ad that we believe will appeal to most voters. And tonight, you will get an exclusive pre-listen before it begins airing tomorrow. Take a listen."

[*An announcer in a very dry and monotone voice speaks.*]

"Are you tired of the other parties' failed attempts at education reform?

Are you growing increasingly concerned about the disparity between the rich and the poor?

Are you fed-up with being ignored by your government?

Well, what are you going to do about it?

Absolutely nothing and in 2008, Neither are we!"

Paid fo' by Po' Folks for Status Quo."

Gasps from the crowd blared loud and clear through the tiny recorder.

"We expect this ad to do well because people don't really want things to change. They just..." Easy pauses, stares into his cup, swirls around its content and finally takes a sip from the glass of water that was left at the podium for the speaker.

"Hey. Wait a minute! Wait a cotton-picking-minute! Who left me some water up here? All of that good stuff behind the bar and y'all put some *water* up here. I thought it was gin or something. Well, I was hoping. But never in a thousand lives would I have thought that you would've left me some water. Ain't that a...what kind of Mickey Mouse operation are you running around..."

[*Easy's words become incomprehensible as the recorder emits a strange scratching sound. The tape-recorder was rubbing against the inside of Bonny's pocket as she jumped out of her seat to get Easy a proper drink of cognac from the bar. Slowly, Easy's voice becomes distinguishable again.*]

Scratch

Scratch

"…turn this place upside down. I don't play around. Alright. Alright now. Thank you Bonny. Now I can continue. What was I saying?"

"People don't want things to change," boomed Bonny's voice from the recorder.

"Yea. Yea. That's it…what was it again?"

"People don't want things to change!"

"That's right. That's right. People don't…ugmm…whatever…I could stand here and lie *Hiccup* to you like all of the others candidates," Easy rambles. "But I'm gonna keep it real. They promise to help the poor and whatever. But I'm going to keep it real…keep it real. That's right. If you're poor today, then after my four years in office you'll still be poor. Yep. That's just how it is; that's how it's been. When I'm done, at least there won't be any surprises, no failed expectations, and no watered-down solutions that wasted tax-payers' money but didn't address the real problems anyway. *Hiccup*

"This is some good stuff you got me Bonny. Well, I guess. You know how after you've had so much to drink even your taste buds turn numb? Anyway...well, I'll tell you one thing. I'll tell you though. You rich, white people sure do contribute to some campaigns. Yep, you sure do, and I need your support. And I know what you like too. I know. As soon as I enter office, I plan to start making your lives better. Yep. I'm going to make your life better by making you feel safe. How? Guess. Nope. I'll tell you...by being tough on crime. And what are my plans for being tough on crime, you ask? I plan to throw more niggas in jail, that's how! You know what? There just aren't enough niggas in jail these days. I'm going to be like, 'Hey you! Yea you darkie. You just won a new car! That blue one over there with the swirling lights on top. It's yours. Now get in the back!' Ha. Ha. Yep. Another day, another black behind bars."

The gasps and awes of the audience began to grow louder and louder until their uproar eventually drowned out Easy on the microphone. Police officers tried to calm down the audience with no avail. Some men even tried to rush the stage and had to be wrestled down in their tuxedos and handcuffed. Easy just stood there — thrilled.

"You see? Yoooou see?" he slurred. "Look at how successful I'd be as Mayor? I ain't even Mayor yet *Hiccup* and I...I caused three black men go to jail."

The audience erupted; pepper spray flooded the air from the back of the auditorium. Easy remained at the podium and watched the chaos ensue with his trademark shoulder shrug of indifference as the cloud of pepper spray slowly crept to the front of the auditorium.

"What? What's the problem? I'm just keeping with the Status Quo. Y'all act like they haven't *been* disproportionately throwing blacks in jail. *Cough* I gotta get out of here. You people are bringing down my buzz, so let me finish. Let me finish! Settle down. Settle down. In 2008, when it comes to running this city, remember...remember, "The Choice B. Easy." *Cough* The Choice B. Easy. *Cough* *Cough*"

[*the tape stops*]

"Do you see, Mr. Easy?" Bonny asks. "It was terrible last night. We barely made it out of there alive."

Snore

"Hello? Mr. Easy?"

Snore

"HELLO!"

"Yea, ugh, yea. Is this Charlene? If this is Charlene, girl I told you I sent that child support check already. And you better not report me this time. Heifer!"

[*Click*]

LOVE & LAUGHTER

EHWWWW

Love is like
a Sun-drenched winter,
engulfed by…
> *Nah, that ain't it.*

Love is like
a seashore breeze,
tickling the…
> *Yea right*

Love is like
picking boogers with…
> *Yeeaaaaa! That's it.*
…no tissue,
one finger
digging deeply; desperately
trying to find
the cause of this strange sensation, taking
all of your attention.

And then,

upon your discovery

you realize the cause

and pause, and simply ask,

"What the *hell* is your purpose?"

No answer.

So like all decent human beings

who rid themselves of worthless things

you flick

and flick

and flick

and flick again

only to realize that there is absolutely

no   way   to get rid of it!

Just like love. *Just like love.*

Now, who wants a taste?

CAN'T WALK AWAY

Twittling 'round my Six-shooter (scratch that…)
Twittling 'round my *TWELVE*-Shooter

                           (my gun is big)

I messed around and
shot myself in the foot.
I knew it would happen
Mama warned me. But I didn't listen
(jus' like I don't listen to my *new* "Mama")
See? I was twittling carelessly. Aimlessly,
fooling around;
you know, thinking…well,
hoping the safety latch was on
But then,

POW!

I shoots myself in the foot.
And it sure hurts like hell.

        like love

               and I still can't walk away…

LIBERATION

Liberation

Liberation!

LI-BE-RA-TION!

My dear, you see how I shout? No doubt - I'm a rebel.

Refusing "The Man's" scraps and

eating at the *head* of the table. So you have to label

me one of the few brothas determined to be,

to be

free

Free!

FREE!

from the oppressive influences of this dreadful society.

ALL its norms I shun. Liberation! and ughmmm.

That's why your marriage proposal hasn't come. Ahh,

Baby,

Come On, You Gotta Buy That! In fact.

I,

ughh,

well,

that was my only comeback.

Yea, I'm determined to be free. But, No. NO!

Not free from you. So beautiful. you are.

But the day after. is the day I'll meet that star.

And it'd be absurd for my word to be

"No" to the Berries of Halle.

Hey. Don't yell at me! Hell, you wanted the truth.

knowing "You can't handle the truth!" Alright,

that was a bit aloof. But…Hey! Where are you going?

My Love? Please!

You'd understand if you could!

Damn!

she's gone.

I guess Liberation ain't always good

Sigh

THE LESSON

1

As if stretched across three rooms, the muscles in the arms showed innate resistance to being pulled in opposite directions with such force. The rib cage bulging through the slender frame arched over an amazing set of stomach muscles contracted in full force to relieve some of the throbbing pressure off the pierced feet. The face, slightly tilted toward the sky, held a grimaced strain of melancholy and defiance while the closed eyes spoke of humble acceptance.

This life-size crucifixion marveled any and every on-looker with its intricate detail. Throughout time, with its painstakingly realistic appearance, the stone-carved statue had taken on a life of its own. Purchased by the Missouri State Penitentiary in the late 1800s, it first began to marvel people when it survived the Great Fire of 1920 and caused a great revival throughout the entire Midwest region.

On a dark and dry August night, a hellacious blaze of orange and yellow scorched the sky while engulfing the entire penitentiary and all of its surrounding fields. For a full thirty-two hours, firefighters struggled to finally subdue the fire that left the twenty-story monstrosity in a great heap of rubble. The building and everything within it was completely destroyed. Well almost. High above the debris, seemingly untouched, was the only structure still recognizable among the wet and charred remains of the building.

The next morning's headline read "He Has Risen…Again." Below the headline was an iconic picture showing the backs of three weary firefighters, still covered in ash and soot, staring up at the crucifix that every witness would later credit with the safe escape of every firefighter, guard, staff, and inmate.

Throughout the remainder of the early- and mid-1900s, the statue received a great deal of attention from scientists who sought to understand its composition, religious scholars who sought to determine its beginnings, and preachers who sought to use it as a tool to convert nonbelievers. After the fire, it was transferred to a neighboring penitentiary and indeed caused a great spike in the number of converts within the prison system. Over time, however, the statue's success in impressing nonbelievers seemed to wane. With His pointy nose and flowing curly hair, many inmates began to stop relating to this statue of Jesus, the Savior.

In 1930, 77 percent of the people admitted to U.S. prisons were white, 22 percent were African American.[1] Within seventy years, by the year 2000, the numbers nearly reversed and African Americans and Latinos accounted for 62.6 percent of all federal and state prisoners.[2] As more and more blacks were incarcerated, the populace of Missouri's penitentiary began to change and the lack of ethnic features on

---

[1] U.S. Department of Justice, Bureau of Justice Statistics, Race of Prisoners Admitted to State and Federal Institutions, 1926-1986, February 1994, p.14, Table 7.
[2] Human Rights Watch, World Report 2002, p.4. These statistics are true. The remainder of the story is fiction.

SLANTED SUBJECTS

Jesus' face soon became a very contentious point of conflict.

"No one really knows for sure," bellowed the voice from the petite figure in the front of the room.

Immaculately dressed in a three-piece, blue suit with simple gold cuff links and an elegant but non-intrusive blue tie, Elwin Rodgers stood. He always stood. It was just one of the noted acts of respect he gave superiors as well as complete strangers. "You never know when you may be entertaining Angels," he would say if people asked him about his peculiar devotion to tact and manners.

When he was first transferred to the penitentiary, due to his unchanging politeness, the warden coined him "Elwin the Chap." Soon after, the entire penitentiary, from the prisoners to the Director, called him by no other name. Although Elwin called everyone by their last name and appropriate title, the majority of people never even knew Elwin's last name to return the gesture. However, it was not out of disrespect or condescension. Elwin was well liked, even amongst the most hardened criminals. And eventually, in a gesture of endearment, the prisoners switched around and abbreviated "Elwin the Chap" to give him a more appropriate name — one that also paid homage to his constant place of worship. They named him "ChapEl."

"No one can really say with one hundred percent certainty," repeated ChapEl as he paced across the front of the penitentiary's "visiting room" turned sanctuary.

With elongated steps that paced with a clatter from his Stetson shoes, each response flowed from his mouth just as gracefully and rhythmically as his walk. Suddenly, he stopped dead in his tracks and quickly faced the twenty-two inmates who were watching him intensely as if they were trying to absorb every word that fell from his lips. Like the tiny oar that moves a ship, ChapEl's soft and polite voice was strong enough to move mountains with its conviction and command over religious matters.

"However, the most important characteristic of Jesus is that He is the Son of God. His race and ethnicity should not matter to any of you."

Not surprised by his sudden stop and serious tone, the inmates continued to watch and listen. They had grown accustomed to ChapEl's dramatic stops. Instead of raising his voice or using profanity, he would turn such pauses into exclamation points at the end of an important sentence.

From the ceiling, the dim glow of cheap lighting produced a grayish haze over everything and everyone. Standing in front of a cascade of gloomy blue tiles that stretched across the entire area, ChapEl faced a spaciously empty room of thirty rust-ridden, black folding chairs that were filled with twenty-two bright orange jumpsuits. He seemed majestic in his surroundings. As he stood beneath the marvelous crucifix that hung as the room's only ornament of decoration (as well as the only distinguishing item that changed the space from a rickety visiting room to a sanctuary), ChapEl seemed to be an exact opposite of the statue's physical features but an undeniable mirror of its temperament.

Instead of thin and flowing hair, ChapEl's hair was short, kinky and receding. Where Jesus was thin and muscular, ChapEl was loose and comfortable. And conflicting with Jesus' pointy nose was ChapEl's wide nostrils that spoke of an African heritage. However, the lack of melanin in ChapEl's skin revealed his ancestors forced infidelity. He, like Jesus, was a descendant of slaves and he, like Jesus, carried their sense of humility, burrowing good nature, and defiant strength.

"Yo El, come on brotha," dismissed a deep voice from the back of the room with gentleness and compassion. It was Joe N. Turner. "His race don't matter? Man, look at that statue behind you. That is, without a doubt, a white man. And me personally, I can't get down wit' praying at the feet of some white, blue-eyed devil. Straight up."

As more than half of the group nodded with agreement, his voice grew more stern and emotional.

"How in the hell can any black man maintain his dignity if he's been enslaved by a white man, had his mother and his wife *raped* by a white man, been thrown in jail by the white man's grandsons…and then…and then come in here and bow down to a *white* savior?! What? It ain't gonna happen, Dog! It just ain't gonna happen."

Surprised by the emotion with which the young man spoke, ChapEl stopped dead in his tracks — this time he stopped without the intent of making a dramatic point in his speech. He realized that this discussion was about more than just the heredity of Jesus Christ. These men harbored deep emotional scars.

With anxious stares awaiting his response, ChapEl decided to try to tackle the issue before the entire class completely turned their backs on Christianity. Although it greatly displeased him to discuss the race of Jesus, he was not going to let something so minor prevent the salvation of souls. Slowly, peacefully, and articulately, El began to pace across the front of the room.

2

"Yes. Mr. Turner," ChapEl began. "Jesus has been depicted as a white man for decades, generations, even centuries. World renowned painters like Rembrandt and Michelangelo have depicted Jesus in such a manner. Yet, times are changing. Many artists are beginning to paint exceptional depictions of a black Jesus. Some of you have probably seen such depictions."

"Yea! That's right!" said Mr. Jefferson, one of the three white men in the room. "On TV the other day I saw this comedian wearing a t-shirt with a black-looking Jesus on the front of it saying 'Jesus is my Homeboy.' I didn't have a problem with it 'cause I wouldn't care if He *was* black. I happen to think black people are–"

"Shut up Cracker!" yelled Joe N. Turner.

He stood up with a look of pure hatred. "You don't interrupt the good doctor when he's speaking. Y'all bastards may run the world out there, but you gone shut the hell up in here! Now if I hear you say one more thing, you're gonna meet your white, blue-eyed Jesus a lot sooner than you might want, understand?"

"Mr. Turner, such exclamations are highly inappropriate," responded ChapEl in a tone equally polite as it was calm. "Everyone has a right to share their stories, opinions, or whatever else they may want to share."

Patiently walking over and extending his hand to the older white male who appeared determined to keep his mouth shut for an eternity, ChapEl continued.

"Mr. Jefferson, you are correct. The black-Jesus-notion has begun to take on a commercial spin for those who seek fashion as a source of rebellion. But do not be fooled into believing that the idea of a black Jesus is popular and/or accepted. Take Renee Cox for example. She became an overnight sensation due to her controversial photo of a black Jesus. Well, she was also naked in the picture, but that's another matter.

"So which one is accurate?" asked ChapEl rhetorically. "That is the conversation all of you want to have, right? Despite my continued attempts to show you that such a question is irrelevant, you all are determined to seek the answer."

"Yea man," spoke a young voice near the front, "it's mad relevant 'cause brothas are sick and tired of being brainwashed...seeing the white man as our master, protector, savior, or whatever else they think they need to be to keep us niggas in check."

"Alright." replied ChapEl, trying to prevent others from joining in and creating a barrage of pent-up comments.

He stood silently.

He closed his eyes and sent a quick prayer to heaven to seek forgiveness if his actions were inappropriate. He did not want to lend credibility to mankind's infatuation with Christ's ethnicity, but he also did not want people to turn away from Christianity because Jesus had been portrayed as a white man.

Finally, he begins.

"Alright. Let's see if we can figure it out. Now, distinguishable descriptions of Jesus are absent in the Bible. However, we may be able to determine his ethnicity by analyzing the race of His ancestors. But even this will be tricky. The Bible does not explicitly give their races or physical descriptions either. Plus, after all of that, we don't know what type of affect being half-God would have on a person's ethnicity. But for your sake, we will try to solve this great mystery.

"Now, if Jesus was the Son of God and the Virgin Mary, we can only trace the ancestors of His mother, right? Alright, let's see here..."

As though the tile floor was his own personal percussion section, ChapEl's pace did not miss a beat while he simultaneously opened his trusty Bible that never ventured too far away from his hand. He quickly turned to Luke.

"Based on her lineage given in Luke 3:23-38, one can study the Old Testament and conclude that Jesus' ancestors included...Well let us do it this way.

We will highlight each of the key people who may shed some light on Jesus' ethnicity, alright?"

The men silently waited for ChapEl to continue. Time and time again throughout his career, ChapEl had to think on his feet and clearly answer any and every question that might prevent persons from becoming converts. Battling short attention spans, he had to be concise. For many inmates, this would be the only time they would ever brave one of the sessions; therefore, ChapEl could never really rely on "Let me find out and I'll get back to you." Yet, despite the pressure, he always seemed capable. Through 15 years of service, he had become exceedingly proficient and thorough in providing exceptional, correct, and convincing answers.

"Let's start with Tamar. In Luke 3:33, it states that Perez was a descendant of the Virgin Mary. Now, if I recall correctly, Perez was the son of Tamar. Yes. Here it is. In Matthew 1:3, it states that Tamar was Perez's mother and also a descendant of Mary.

"This is of importance to Jesus' ethnicity because Tamar was a Canaanite from the line of Ham, and most scholars agree that Ham is the father of black persons. He was one of the three sons of Noah who repopulated the earth after the Flood and he is believed to be black because scripture notes him as the father of the Egyptians in Psalms 105:23, 106:22, and 78:51. You all are familiar with and know that the Ancient Egyptians were black, right?"

As he awaited a response from the group, he felt a tiny drop hit the top of his head. He stopped in his tracks and looked up but there was no leak in the roof. He stared for a period long enough to confuse the inmates. They did not know what point he was trying to make with such a long pause. They thought it was another one of his pauses of exclamation.

But as he stood there, staring upward near the spot that should have held the leak, ChapEl found himself staring at the face of the crucifix. To him, it seemed impossible, but the liquid undoubtedly had fallen from the crucifix's right eye.

Touching the top of his head where the wet spot remained, ChapEl pulled back his index finger and was shocked to see what appeared to be blood. As the reality began to churn in his mind, his eyes widened. Without blinking, the thought gripped him as he stood there staring at the stone structure. Slowly, he turned away from the crucifix and toward the inmates.

His once light-skinned face struck stark white. His eyes became bewildered and afraid as though he had witnessed a ghost walk across his path.

The inmates all sat there and watched as if glued to their chairs with their mouths open.

ChapEl was trying to tell them something. But, as if an immovable lump was lodged in his throat, he could not speak. He just stood there, stark white with his hands on his throat and his mouth gapping open like a cat whose hairball wouldn't fall.

Suddenly, ChapEl's eyes shot away from the inmates and began to look straight ahead to the back wall of blue tile. As though he was in a trance, without taking his eyes off the wall, his face finally untied into a relative calm. He slowly began to lift his right arm. Slowly, he lifted his arm until it was completely vertical.

His index finger pointed at the crucifix.

Straight ahead, red beams shot out of the eyes of the stone Jesus. The inmates, the most hardened criminals, fell to the floor face-first. Tears struck down every face as they all began to speak in tongues and prophesize. No longer lit by fluorescent lights and covered by blue tiles, the entire room was blanketed with a deep red that appeared wet but clung to the scene with no streaks and no waves.

The color soaked into everything and everyone. Turning to face the wall behind them and kneeling in their places, all of the bowed heads of the prisoners began to lift with precision. Their eyes opened towards the wall opposite of the crucifix. With everyone facing the same direction, they all stared at the same wall.

They all began to see through the same set of eyes:

The eyes of Jesus.

3

They all face the same wall and the sight is clear.

The vision is clear:

Water stains are the only decoration in a rundown, one-bedroom apartment where a flickering television set sits on top of a milk crate in the middle of the floor. It is the only source of light and it castes a blue hue of melancholy across the stench of mildew that rises from every corner. A flickering newscast switches to static, back to the newscast, and back to static. Underneath the dingy blinds of the apartment's small window breaches an intruding red light.

[*News Anchorman*]

"Mysteriously, the sky seems to have turned a deep red and…

Static

…dumbfounded scientists. Such an event is unprecedented and the State Governor has asked for everyone to remain calm…

Static

…take you live to the streets where it seems everyone is right now…

Static

…anything happens, our cameras will keep you live and…

Static

Static

Static

"INSTEAD, ONE OF THE SOLDIERS PIERCED JESUS' SIDE WITH A SPEAR, BRINGING A SUDDEN FLOW OF BLOOD AND WATER." John 19:34

Through the blinds and outside the window, scattered gray clouds drown in a dense red that covers the entire sky. Midday humidity hovers over the city and the heat begins to agitate because the apartment does not convenience with air conditioning, nor does a visible sun explain the rise in temperature. So reminiscent of blood is the color of the sky that one expects it to bleed.

And it does.

Thick Red Rain falls from the sky and begins to cover the earth. It's heavy and one begins to hear the sound of screeching cars below the apartment window. There is no visibility to be had on any car windshield and even our small, apartment window becomes covered with the flowing, red rain. The sky can no longer be seen.

Running down the stairs and standing in front of the crusty front door of the apartment complex with its peeling tan paint, one can view millions of people standing outside. The entire city is soaked.

Then, just as quickly as it started, the rain stops. The sky opens with a bright beam of light. With the strength of ten suns, its brightness of pure white makes the beam unbearable by sight. Seven white doves fly from the sky to the earth.

The light begins to dim and people immediately fall to their knees. Too shocked to utter final prayers, they just watch with unblinking eyes. It is uncontested. This is the Second Coming.

"BUT THE LORD SAID TO SAMUEL, 'DO NOT CONSIDER HIS APPEARANCE OR HIS HEIGHT...THE LORD DOES NOT LOOK AT THE THINGS MAN LOOKS AT. MAN LOOKS AT THE OUTWARD APPEARANCE, BUT THE LORD LOOKS AT THE HEART.'" 1 Samuel 16:7

Inside the dimming beam of light, on the earth, a form begins to appear. Clumped dirt and clay begin to rise from the ground and give form to flesh. A slender figure, attractive but not dominating, slowly begins to walk from the glaring light. Naked without shame, he walks barefoot over the red-soaked earth with closed eyes.

Immediately, people begin to run towards him with hopeful desperation in their eyes. Trampling the slow, elderly and young, mobs of people rush the walking figure and threaten to trample Him due to their speed. A force seems to beckon each person from their insides and no legs seem to tire as people run for blocks, even miles. As they quickly approach at unfathomable and reckless speeds, His head slowly begins to rise.

As if stopped by an unseen wall, the front runners stop in mid-stride. Their front leg simply stops beside the following leg. Standing vertically, instantly, and absolutely, they are all within arms reach of Him. No one dares touch. They simply await His instruction.

It never comes.

Whew! I guess Christianity was the right religion. I'm glad I picked the right one. I feel sorry for Hauk-beem and his Muslim friends over there. I don't know why they ran over here. Don't try to switch teams now! Rushing my Jesus, you must be crazy. You might as well prepare for your life in hell!

He isn't as big and strong as I expected. I'm actually bigger than he is. Surely, I will become a major, general or something important in His army. I may even become His right hand man!

He is more beautiful than any portrait has ever depicted him. He is certainly the epitome of man and beauty. I can practically see heaven in His deep blue eyes. With such a small nose and curly hair, he is the most beautiful white man I have ever seen.

I can't believe He's black! I bet you these white people are bugging out! That's what they get. All this time they've been praising Jesus, they've been praising a black man! Look at his flat-nose and kinky hair. Only a black man can stand in front of millions of people butt-naked with such confidence. Gone 'head Jesus!

Oh my God, Jesus is a woman! I knew those historians had changed history to suit their own sexist notions. Man is so weak-minded and simple. But now, no man will be able to refute the dominance of woman.

My dream has come true. I knew it. Jesus is Asian...
YES! Jesus is gay...

Jesus is handicapped...

Jesus is...

Jesus...

"MY DEAR BROTHERS, TAKE NOTE OF THIS: EVERYONE
SHOULD BE QUICK TO LISTEN, SLOW TO SPEAK..."
James 1:13

Everyone waited for their Jesus to lead the
world to glory. But He only stood there. His eyes
closed. His mouth closed. He listened to the hearts of
His people. Everyone maintained smiles from ear to
ear. Glee filled each and every one of their hearts.
With their deepest desires fulfilled, they all eagerly
awaited the opportunity to follow *their* Jesus who
validated their own importance.

Smiling largely, an older black woman could
no longer hold in her happiness. "Hallelujah!" she
screamed. "Hallelujah! THANK you Father!"

"Praise Him Sister," replied a youthful black
man with an athletic build and bald head. "Praise our
Black Messiah! The Savior of the *World*!"

"Black Messiah? What are you talking about young fella? Jesus is as white and pure as the undriven snow."

"Who are you looking at? Jesus is clearly Asian..."

"Jesus is not Asian! How could the Savior be Asian? *Why* would the Savior be Asian?"

"It's better that He be Asian than White! How could the Savior come from such an oppressive group of people?"

"How could He be Asian? Blacks pioneered spirituality throughout antiquity. Of course it would be fitting for Him to be Black!"

"Are you all blind as well as crazy? He is a She! Women are the most humble creatures walking the earth. Everyone knows that God abhors arrogance and man is just about as close to pure arrogance as a person can be. Jesus is standing before all of us in all of Her beauty and glory. This is the most explicit, irrefutable, and final showing to all of you sexist liars!"

"Jesus? As a woman? You're crazy!"

"You're dumb if you think..."

"That's impossible…"

"Who would follow such a Savior?"

"Finally! We truly know that the dominant people are…"

"Hell no! God's chosen people are…"

"We're obviously the closest to His heart!"

[*Inaudible Screams*]

The talking turns to yelling. The yelling turns to screams. The screaming becomes unbearably loud.

Everyone screams.

No one listens.

The debate becomes heated and punches are thrown. Knives are pulled. Guns are drawn.

No one notices Jesus walking away.

"WHEN JESUS SAW THIS, HE WAS INDIGNANT. HE SAID TO THEM, 'LET THE LITTLE CHILDREN COME TO ME, AND DO NOT HINDER THEM, FOR THE KINGDOM OF GOD BELONGS TO SUCH AS THESE. I TELL YOU THE TRUTH, ANYONE WHO WILL NOT RECEIVE THE KINGDOM OF GOD LIKE A LITTLE CHILD WILL NEVER ENTER IT.'"
Mark 10:14-15

In the midst of the madness, Jesus gathers the children who are too young to understand what is going on. They are too young to fight for the strength, the importance, and the superiority of *their* people.

"BY THE TIME LOT REACHED ZOAR, THE SUN HAD RISEN OVER THE LAND. THEN THE LORD RAINED DOWN BURNING SULFUR ON SODOM AND GOMORRAH – FROM THE LORD OUT OF THE HEAVENS." Genesis 19:23

The glaring light maintains a hold onto Jesus and the children. They walk away, leaving the adults in darkness. Without looking back to face the spectacle, Jesus weeps. Outside of the beam of light, the red sky falls upon the earth.

Everything is nothing. no more.

SPIRITUAL BARS

BAPTISM

I

for the Reborn, past faults shed off like skin

shed Sin to shed Light. Within

      a soul tapped

with vocals of harp strings

Blaring the colors of nectarine

orange, sky blue, and deep red

seeking attention to mention its Source:

THE MOST HIGH

CREATOR OF VOCAL PALETTES AND RAINBOWS

whispering, "Your *mind* you must close.

For the truth you seek only appears in the *ears* of the

Holy"

II

so Rising from Holy Water,

my body/mind/spirit began to surface

proclaiming life's purpose:

Gather 'round. Gather the color of vibration

Gather sound. deep down

within

       where God beckons

              …and obey

LISTENING & LEARNING

One day, way before I learned to talk

and be "educated"

I felt the sound of a cool breeze

lecturing on the purpose of existence.

Chirping birds silenced with anticipation.

They wanted to see if I too would listen.

I did not

"I am Man. *Sole Teacher of Knowledge & Truth.*

With Open Mouth and Closed Ears,

I named you all through the years.

So what could you possibly teach me?

Absolutely nothing."

So I thought…

Today, as the breeze blows

still, I search for the purpose of life.

Arrogantly,

overlooking the lesson of how the wind simply does

what God commands

without fail.

without question.

And I will probably die without knowing

why I have lived

A life-long search wasted. Blinded

Blinded

by self-importance

BLUE DESERT

1

Each day

a seed is planted in the desert's sand.

Beneath the shoeless soles of burned feet

turned black and grey

Tattered

and dingy

cloth cling to bones

of aged and shelterless.

Stooping

and planting. with No water.

No soil. No sun.

Only Hope nurtures the tiny seeds,

constantly rubbed in

and prayed over

rubbed in and

prayed over

day after

day after

years of planting,

the planter finds

that nothing but frustration grows.

   Nothing but frustration grows!

and he fills the air with justified and

contemptuous complaints

curses the ground. curses God.

2

But one day, after prayer, after

prayer after

prayer after

frustration dies

The sound of shuffling sand

replaces the sound of the planter's constant complaints.

In the Dark Silence of the Blue Desert

above the sound of the shuffled, infertile sand

the cloudless sky recognizes the faint and tired voice

of the planter's worship

the planter's Praise.

      Simply saying

Thank you Lord.

Thank you for the seeds.

.

THE FUNDRAISER

1

"Young man, what is that fragrance you wear?" asked a petite and pale lady well into her eighties. "That scent is so familiar. I'd recognize it anywhere. It's the exact same cologne my father used to wear before he passed away. I was so young! I've searched everywhere for that exact scent. Please tell me where you got it!"

Easy looked over the woman with a face of pure enjoyment.

"Ma'am, this ain't nothing but some Brut on top of a cognac hangover…well, mixed in with some cheap perfume. I had some *friendly* company before I came over, if you know what I mean," he chuckled.

The woman appeared disturbed.

Easy appeared indifferent.

"Well, maybe you don't. Do you know if your father used to go down to Willie's Freak Hut, or was he an upscale, Paradise Palace kind of man? Me? I like Willie's Freak Hut myself. I sho…"

Suddenly, the old woman clasped her hands together and began to gasp for air. Chills shot up and down her curled spine with every sentence Easy uttered.

Bonny just shook her head and watched the destruction unfold. With every passing second, the elder lady's wrinkles seemed to sink in deeper and Bonny could have sworn that she saw the one black strand of hair on the woman's head streak gray.

"I'm just Keeping it Real!" said Easy with the tone of a polished politician. The old woman sat in her chair sobbing silently in her hands while Easy stood above her in his dark blue suit and red power tie (Bonny had brought the clothes with her and made Easy change out of his short, short khaki shorts and brown sandals with black socks pulled up to his knees).

Full of his usual, over-inflated ego, he stood with his chest puffed out, chin up and hands on his hips as if he just saved the world. He is completely oblivious to the fact that the old woman's tears are not tears of joy.

In a quick attempt to distract the rest of the women who began to gather around the saddened lady, Bonny began to tell a story about the time she was on *The Price Is Right*. And it worked. The old women were in an instant trance. Like little girls, their eyes lit up as Bonny started to describe Bob Barker.

Over the summer, Bonny had learned how to save Easy from great mobs and she knew the quickest way to grab the attention of an entire group of old, retired white women was to either talk about Soap Operas, Oprah, or the man of their dreams, Bob Barker. With white hair that sat on his head like a crown of nobility, and tailored suits that fit his aged-but-firm body perfectly, Bob was their supermodel — the supermodel of the elderly. He had caused each and every one of them to moisten their bloomers at some point in time.

"Does he look as good in person as he does on TV?" asked one curious woman.

"I heard those little Pop Tart hostesses were showing him more than what was behind Door #1, if you catch my drift."

"Well, I can't blame them. He can 'Cum on down' on me anytime!"

"Martha!"

"You're so naughty!"

They all giggled frantically like schoolgirls. Bonny had shown the women their only way back to youth: sexual fantasy. Scanning across the room from left to right, one could see nothing but all-out, hysterical fun. There was nothing but smiles, grins, cocked-back heads of laughter, looks of longing, looks of nostalgia, and Easy...with his head in the trash container.

"Oh my God," exclaimed Easy as he partially lifted his head from the trash. "I had a mental picture and I...I think I'm gonna be sick...Curse it...my imagination!"

With nonstop blinking eyes, a sweaty brow and a grayish-blue face, Easy runs outside as quickly as his feet would carry him.

I need some fresh air and a drink after that. Don't these women have any manners? Goodness gracious. Forget about asking for campaign money, I need to give them a talk on etiquette!

Running to the car, he finds his secret stash of bourbon under the driver's seat. *Trusty flask, don't fail me now. You've always done a good job of ridding memories, and this is certainly one I want to forget.* *Sigh* *Bob Barker...and...and...Martha...* "Oh my God! I did it again! Lord have mercy!"

[*Ten minutes pass*]

Finally, returning to the party and looking across the variety of smiling faces, Easy wanted to kick himself. They were all wrinkled and pale. It seemed that the only variant was the color of their puffy afros, ranging from midnight blue to hazy purple. Easy remembered the sistas on the bus stops in the inner-city with their fluorescent color wigs and realized that these old women were more "Ghetto Fabulous" than they probably would care to know.

I should have known there would be no cute chicks here. This ain't no woman's league. This is a granny's league...a we're-all-about-to-croak league...a two-steps-outta-the-grave league...a...I'm tapped out...no creativity. Oh well. At least they stopped talking about sex. This is going to be a long day. I got it! I'll just find the bathroom and keep ducking in there. That'll make time go by faster. Looka there. Alright! I bet you she's *headed to the bathroom. Prune juice running through you, huh Granny? She must be...Oh my God. I can't believe I just...Damn male reflexes! I just looked at her booty.* *Shudder* *Ehwww. Old lady booty! Curse it...my eyes!*

Easy runs back out of the front door.

He returns ten minutes later — this time a little tipsy.

Carrying a wooden tray of Iced Tea, the host of the Fundraiser walks in from the kitchen. Standing at about 4'7'', she has on an apron that says, "I don't really cook. My husband bought this as a HINT!" She smiles a smile of welcome. "Hello everyone," she said to all of her guest. "I see that one of our very special guests has already arrived. Welcome, Mr.

Easy. We have heard that you have decided to run for Mayor. Now usually, we only raise money for the local high school, the summer soccer league, one of Marge's surgeries; things like that. However, this year we have received a number of odd applications, including yours. I guess the economy has dried up a lot of other sources for individuals, but we are happy to consider each and every application."

"Mrs. White, it is my pleasure to be herre," slurred Easy as he stood to take the tray from his host. "Let me…let me get that for you," he says as he wobbles the tray and nearly spills the tea on everyone.

"No. No. Mr. Easy, that is quite alright. Maybe I should just sit the tray over here next to Betty."

"Oh. Well, alright then. Hey Betty, when you're fixing my tea make sure mines 'Long Island,' if you know what I mean."

Without being prompted, Easy walks to the center of the room to deliver his speech. "Now, most people would ask, 'What is a black man like you doing in this old, suburban, white woman's house?' And, I'd tell them straight up, 'That's a good question 'cause I ain't here borrowing sugar.'"

Hiccup

The elder ladies looked at one another with glances of nervousness.

"Nope, I'm here 'cause I'm running for Mayor of this great city and black people just don't seem to donate to political campaigns for some reason. Well, I guess they got better things to do with their money — like eat!

"Oh, and play the lotto," he chuckled.

[*Pause*]

Easy just stands there — blinking and grabbing his crotch.

"Hold on. Hold on ladies. I gotta piss like you wouldn't believe. Do you think the lady with the yellow afro is done in there?"

[*Five minutes later*]

"Whew. Alright. Boy that was a great piss. You know how sometimes a piss can be so good your body shakes? It was one of those! Hey, I saw your Martha Stewart magazine in there. I love Martha

Stewart. *Hiccup* I do. Don't look like that. Martha Stewart is one of my favorite role models. Before I started watching her show, I used to go to clubs and spend all my money on drinks. But not anymore. Naw! She taught me how to economize. Now I buy all of my booze in big, family-size jugs at warehouse prices and get drunk before I even go to the club. I've become so thrifty that I even sneak in a few cans of beer just in case some chick wants me to buy her a drink. I just sit back all cool and then 'Bam,' I slam a can of beer in front of her. 'Hey Baby, I'm Easy.'"

Scratching his head in wonder, "I can't really say it's been very effective though, but hey, I've saved thousands!"

Bonny dropped her head in disbelief, and Easy just smiled and shrugged his usual shoulder-shrug of indifference. His eyes spoke of tipsy confidence.

"Ughmm. You said you get drunk *before* you go to the club," asked a nervous looking, old woman with a dusty-orange afro. Her head slightly bobbled side to side in a constant state of shake as she slowly uttered, "Does that…does that mean you drive while intoxicated?"

The question caught Easy off guard and the entire house watched and waited for his answer. "Drive while intoxicated? Drive while intoxicated?" Easy repeated to buy himself time to think. It was the typical male tactic when being prodded by a woman.

"Do I drive while intoxicated?"

For the first time this evening, his eyes gave way to a hint of worry. It was not that he cared about telling them the truth — not at all. He liked to keep it real. It's just that the woman's look of nervousness reminded him that he was in the suburbs, and anytime Easy found himself surrounded by older-white women, he always became paranoid and easily excited.

This is all my Mama's fault! She should have never made me join the boy scouts.

2

Easy began to think back to the time he was a young boy who loved to play and destroy things. To help him find something useful to do with his time during the summer, his mother made him join the local boy scouts. The very first lesson of chivalry that was taught to the young boys was to make sure they helped old women cross the street. This lesson would soon come to haunt Easy and alter his behavior for the rest of his life.

One bright Sunday afternoon, Easy was walking to Mrs. Johnson's house, otherwise known as "the Candy Lady." She didn't work. She just sold bootleg candy and hot pickles to all the kids within a 15 block radius. Of course, she was also the wife of Stan, the local dentist.

Two blocks away from his destination, Easy noticed an old, white woman struggling with her Sunday groceries. Stooped over in her pink and orange, plaid one-piece dress and tall socks, she dragged her frail metal cart of groceries on two wheels.

Easy remembered the voice of his Scout master: "Never, *ever* let a struggling old woman cross your path without helping her. Any Boy Scout worth his badge lives for the moment to help the elderly." This being his first opportunity to fulfill his Scout's duty, Easy ran over towards the old woman with a huge grin.

"Ma'am, let me take your groceries," he said with a little bass in his voice to imitate his Scout master's voice of responsibility.

Startled, the old woman quickly jumped to the other side of her cart. It happened so fast that it surprised Easy. Then, with the metal cart between them and with a look of nervousness, she pleaded, "Son, all I have are prunes and bottles of V8. Why don't you just steal directly from the grocer like the other little black boys?"

With that said, she took her cart in her right hand and waddled slowly across the street. Despite her snail pace, she made it across the street with ease and Easy didn't know whether she made it across the street so effortlessly because she really didn't need his help, or if she was running from him and that was just the fastest she could go. Either way, he knew his Boy Scout days were done. Well, so he thought. His mother still made him go for the rest of the summer.

Now, Easy saw the same nervousness in this old, white lady, and he stood dumbfounded and speechless just like the day he stood on that corner — two blocks away from "the Candy Lady."

"I, ugmmm," stuttered Easy. "I–"

Suddenly the door bell rang.

"Thank God."

It was the other applicant.

3

Looking the young man up and down, Easy was pleased to have the distraction. However, he also knew that the guest was his competition and threatened his chances of winning the $150,000 the winner was poised to win. Easy was determined to give this youngster the hardest time of his life.

Standing at about 5'2'', the new guest held a face of reservation and uncertainty. A frail and young black man of about 22 years of age, he was dressed in scraggily jeans, some run over Doc Martins, and a black t-shirt with the square root of π written on the front in plain white letters.

"Hello everyone," said the new addition to the festivities. "I'm sorry for being late but I had to catch the bus and the closest it would drop me off wasn't close at all. I guess not enough people from the city come to the suburbs, so I apologize in advance if I smell like 'outside' for I had to walk a long way and the sun rides you like a cowboy does a dead bull out there. I would love something to drink."

The old women around the room looked at him with a look of fascination. They really didn't know what to make of him and his unorthodox speaking style. Although he did not wear a shirt and tie like Easy, they didn't consider him to be threatening-looking. Therefore, although he was a bit of an oddity, he was welcome.

Seeing the arrival of her second guest, Mrs. White scampered to the front door. She was just as relieved by the distraction as Easy. "Everyone, this is Mr. Kemet," she fumbled. Flashing Kemet a nervous smile, Mrs. White quickly handed him a glass of ice tea and tried to smooth over the awkward moment created by Easy's speech. She slowly walked Kemet towards the only vacant seat in the house. She had everything planned perfectly — everything — from the time, to the food, to the tea, to the number of seats.

She was a perfectionist, and she ran Jerry's Geriatrics with an astounding attention to detail that made every event a success. This event, however, seemed to be headed to the pits and she was determined to salvage what was left.

Jerry's Geriatrics was a rather new organization to the city. Looking to ride on the popularity of Jerry's Kids, the group was initially formed in 1996 to raise money for elders in need. The organization soon became a huge success, and because it was so effective, the group expanded its mission to include fundraising for other matters. This year, however, for their philanthropy drive, the members were surprised to receive applications for a number of things other than the typical request for one of Marge's annual surgeries. They received that request as well, but this year they also received an application to support Po' Folks for Status Quo and an application to provide research money for the study of social progress and regress.

"Alright. Is everyone taken care of?" asked Mrs. White with a grin of absolute pleasantry. "Good.

Alright. We will allow both of you to explain your need for the money, how it will be used, and why you believe your need trumps the needs of the other applicants. Since you have already started Mr. Easy, we will ask that you continue. Then, we will have Mr. Kemet explain his need."

"Alright. Let me clear my throat."

Without turning away from the crowd, Easy coughs and clears his throat in the most disturbing manner. Bonny could have sworn she saw particles fly from his mouth into Martha's glass of tea.

"Good afternoon ladies and gentleman. My name is Stevie B. Easy and I'm running for Mayor. Now, I know other black politicians have turned you off in the past, but let me start by saying that I ain't nothing like them. First of all, I'm not a Democrat. I'm an Independent. Second of all, honestly, to be truthful, I'm scared of white folks."

Everyone's face scrunched up in disbelief as they looked at one another with concern.

"That's right. I said it," Easy smiled, "it's the truth."

Kemet, who already had his misgivings about politicians, could not believe his ears. He knew politicians would say whatever people wanted to hear, but this was out of control. Kemet tried to sit still, but his facial expression of tightened lips, and narrow eyes yelled at a disturbing level, "You sellout, Uncle Tom!"

"Now, don't get it confused," continued Easy. "I don't mean that I won't whoop a white boy's tail. I ain't scared of y'all like that. Naw, see? I ain't scared of y'all individually. I'm scared of y'all collectively...especially when I'm surrounded by you. Like...like when I'm in...the suburbs, you know?"

Easy's smile quickly disappeared and small beads of sweat began to collect on his forehead as he scanned the room. Everyone fell silent as they watched the sweating politician twitch as he talked about his fear. Bonny's face, again, fell into her hands.

"I'm serious. Something ain't quite right with white people as a whole. I may not be the smartest brotha in the world, but I got good enough sense to be afraid, for real. E'erybody know that white people do far more drugs in this country than blacks, but...but for some reason blacks are thrown in jail far more often than whites for drug possession."

[*Pause*]

Easy's eyes quickly dart back and forth with nervousness. He continues with great unease, "*Now* tell me I'm crazy. And. And. People of color age way more gracefully and beautifully than whites, right? But for some reason blacks always seem to die twenty years before white people do. Am I lying? Look at you Granny, yea you in the floral dress with your teeth out. You're probably thirty years old, ain't you?

"You see what I'm talking about? Something just ain't right! Let me think...let me think. Alright...here's another one. White folks be always backtalking and badmouthing the police, right? Y'all throw all sorts of tantrums, yell, scream and cuss, tell ya daddy, sue the department, everything. *But,* blacks are the *only ones* always caught on tape getting our heads bashed in."

Easy just dropped his head and shook it from side to side in disbelief. Then, suddenly, he looked up and smiled a huge smile.

"But, that don't mean I won't be a good representative for your interests. No Ma'ams. I still like white people. In fact, I was just telling Bonny the other day how much I love George W. Bush."

The old women, already traumatized by Easy's comments, looked at one another in disbelief. *Could he have anything more outlandish and inappropriate to say?*

Bonny was clutching the arms of her chair as if she was on a roller-coaster ride. Knowing that Easy was just warming up, she anticipated the feeling of her stomach jumping into her throat — or some old lady's pacemaker jumping onto the floor.

"As a matter of fact, I completely disagree with Maya Angelou. Bill Clinton wasn't the first black President. Nah. George W. Bush is the *real* first black President. You better believe it!"

"Ughmm, excuse me speaker." It was Kemet — looking terribly disturbed. And he wasn't the only one. "Please pardon my interruption, but there in your statement lies many fallacies and sketchy rationale that must be addressed before you continue. Do you understand the implications behind your concession that Bush is the first *black* President?"

As he spoke and thought more about the ridiculous statement and the tom foolery being displayed in front of these old women, his voice grew more and more stern. He was disgusted with Easy's speech and he was disgusted with George W. Bush — and it was becoming more and more evident with each sentence he uttered. "Surely you realize that the U.S. Armed Forces are disproportionately comprised of minorities? Those are your brothers and sisters Mr. Bush sent to fight an unprecedented and unjustified war. *Your* Mr. Bush has fought against Affirmative Action, and *your* Mr. Bush refused to even meet with the Congressional Black Caucus and the NAACP. And this...this is who you believe represents Black America?! What's the matter with you? Are you crazy?"

"Are you unstable?" asked Easy with a sinister grin. "Do you always yell at respectable people? Are you on drugs, Kemet? Huh?"

"What?"

"Your Mama. Did she do drugs too? Did she teach you how to use 'em?"

"What?!" snapped Kemet. "What are you talking about? Are you calling my mother a drug addict?"

"That's what I said."

"That's it!"

That was the last straw. Boiling with anger, Kemet stood to his feet ready to fight with every strand in his puny little muscles. Even with the most peaceful of black men, the line is crossed when you talk about their mothers. He stared at Easy with a look of pure fire and advanced toward him with his crusty Doc Martins pounding hatred into the floor with every step. His nostrils flared and his breathing was short and strong.

Short and strong.

Short and…

Short…

and…

He fell — gasping for air.

It was his asthma.

He grabs his inhaler and inhales the medicine like Pookey did his crackpipe in *New Jack City*.

Dang it, you nerd, thought Easy. *You're not even man enough to swing on me so Mrs. White can throw you out and award me the money. Alright then, I'll just have to win it the old fashioned way.*

To the astonishment of the women, Easy just steps over the squirming Kemet and continues his speech. "Alright. Like I was saying before. George W. is the real first black president. The man was caught drinking and driving, first of all. And then…and then, the man was caught doing drugs, smoking weed — everything!"

Easy's face lit up as bright as two million stars. His excitement was evident and uncontainable. "Honestly, for real, he's like part of my family based on those things alone. Only my cousin, 3 Strikes Stan, has a worse record. Plus, the man loves sports, doesn't get up until about 11 a.m., and on top of all of that, spends all the government's money before he even gets it. Now ladies, if that ain't nigga stuff, I don't know what is. And trust me, I know nigga stuff.

"But anyway, I gotta be honest with you. What really inspires me is that my English ain't all that good either. You know, after the whole Ebonics thing, I thought you white people really felt strongly about Americans knowing proper English. Psshht, boy was I wrong. That ain't the case at all. I forgot most of y'all don't know it either. So, I figure if Bush can become President of the United States, then I know I can become Mayor of this great city. And ladies, you can help me. You can be a part of this great movement with your organization's donation. Ladies, the 'Choice B. Easy.'"

Dead silence followed Easy as he walked to his seat with his patented swagger of confidence. All of their mouths were open and no one moved or said a word. So quiet was the silence that Bonny swore no one was even breathing. Kemet still sat on the floor with his back against the wall. He had regained his breathe, but after such a presentation, he was knocked breathless again.

All of the women stared at each other and waited, hoping a camera crew would fall out of the coat closet and pronounce this whole ordeal a joke. This must have been staged, they thought. But, to their dismay, there was no such camera crew. This was really happening.

Slowly, Mrs. White walks away from the telephone. She concludes that the fiasco is over and that she may not need to call the police after all. She was afraid when Kemet stood up to fight, but she now knew that Easy was her biggest threat. Her event, for the very first time was now, officially ruined.

It can't get any worst, she thought. *We might as well finish and get them both the hell out of here.* She moves toward the center of the living room. She doesn't really know what to say.

"Ughmmm. The food should be ready. Let's eat for about ten minutes and hurry this thing along."

* *

One year later, after a humiliating loss, Stevie B. Easy gives his concession speech, which is covered by the local news.

Local, third-party candidate for mayor, Stevie B. Easy, gave his concession speech today. Although the new mayor, Democrat Stan Quo, has held the office for the past two months, Mr. Stevie B. Easy has finally conceded and was quoted as saying the following:

"This is 2000 Florida all over again. I demanded a recount because I just couldn't believe that I had received less than .0000001% of the city's votes. I had a surefire plan for victory. But now, now I understand that the people of this city have spoken and they have said that they do not support Po' Folks for Status Quo. With their votes, they have told the world that only a rich, white man can have a criminal record, be lazy, be inarticu…artic… don't speak good, and still be able to win elections. After this election, I surely have to question, like all of you should, the *equality* in this country? Why can't a black man, with the same characteristics be successful? You hypocritical heathens! You no longer have to worry about me. I'm done with politics. I've been offered a prestigious position at Enron where my talents can be better used."

Mr. Stevie B. Easy is currently being investigated by the IRS for the mismanagement of his campaign funds. However, despite his legal woes, a spokesperson for Enron said, "Mr. Easy is a perfect fit for big business. He has shown us that he can appropriately handle Enron finances with the same care that they have been handled in the past. We welcome him to our New Investments Department, or as he likes to call it:

the Hustle Room.

4

```
┌─────────────────────────────────────────┐
│                                         │
│            KEMET                        │
│        THINKER FOR HIRE                  │
│                                         │
│                  H. 215-THI-NKER        │
│                  C. 267-FOR-HIRE        │
│                                         │
│  ing outside the box.                   │
│                                         │
└─────────────────────────────────────────┘
```

"It has certainly been a pleasure talking with you Mr. Kemet. I have never met anyone quite like you before, and I adore the business cards. Your 'Thinking outside the box' concept is so original. How effective have they been?" asked Mrs. White while she finished the last bite of her turkey sandwich.

"Yea, Kemet, how effective have they been?" asked Easy with a tone of sarcasm as he stared at the young man's worn shoes. "Especially since you seem to be so well-off and everything?"

"Well, honestly, I must admit that they have not been very effective," Kemet replied disappointedly. "I sent my résumé and some business cards to Washington though. I figured if anyone was in desperate need of a thinker, it was the White House. Based on their exasperate need, I expect a hurried call very soon."

Trying to avoid another incident like earlier, Mrs. White steps in. *If they go at it again, Martha is likely to pull out her stun gun, trip over somebody, and shock herself.*

"Alright Kemet. Are you ready to present your material?" asked Mrs. White. "The women have been ever so interested in your request."

Setting down his plate, still full of food, he shrugs his shoulders. During his conversation with Mrs. White, as usual, he had dominated the conversation with his elaborate explanations about any- and everything. He talked so long and explained so many points that he had barely touched his food while Mrs. White had ample time to finish her entire snack.

"Sure.   If everyone else is done eating," answered Kemet.

"Everyone else finished a long time ago," snickered Easy. "Maybe if you'd stop yapping, we could move on with the program. I've been ready to go ever since I found out there was no Long Island in my tea."

Walking to the middle of the living room, Kemet felt at home. Although he looked timid at times, he relished for opportunities to explain his theories and ideas to other people. Although quite jittery while talking to women his age and overwhelmed when threatened by men, he spoke with eloquence when discussing his ideas.

"Ladies and, ughmmm, you Mr. Easy, I humbly present to you a concept that could revolutionize the way we look to move our society. So please feel free to inquire at any time during the presentation. If further elaboration is needed on any point, I will be greatly pleased to answer any questions because it is an indication of mental absorption on the part of the audience."

"I have a point of clarification," interrupted Easy in his most academic voice.

"Already Mr. Easy?"

"I heard you tell Mrs. White that you're a 'thinker' of some sort, right?"

"That is correct."

"Then what were you thinking when you put that outfit together? Who dresses you? Mr. Magoo?"

Everyone in the room chuckled under their breath and Easy felt good that the audience was on his side instead of Kemet's.

"Ok. I will feel greatly honored to entertain questions from anyone but Mr. Easy."

"That ain't fair! You think my questions will be too hard for ya? You can't handle the heat?" he taunted.

"Anyway ladies," Kemet continues. "In these days and times, one of the most fundamentally destructive problems of the world is man's inability to discern progress from regress. We can all agree that mankind has acquired a great deal of knowledge as exemplified in our space travel, cloning discoveries and profound works of art. However, we have yet to produce an effective tool to determine whether our execution and utilization of such knowledge is for the advancement or the destruction of our species. What we lack is a practical gauge, a universal indicator of some sort that judges the progressive or regressive nature of all events, theories, and actions.

"This practical gauge is what I wish to create because once such a tool is established, then mankind will undoubtedly begin its steady transcendence to utopia because this perfect state is the ever-elusive goal of all social endeavors. With such enormous potential, you can understand why funding such a project is worthwhile, and the exceptional news is that I have already formulated a hypothesis that seems to be the key to our problems — the very same problems that we have tried to defeat with ethics, religion, morality, communism, and capitalism. Ladies, I have tested and concluded that 'perfection' is mankind's best indicator of progress and regress."

"But, Mr. Kemet, what exactly is perfect in this world for you to compare?" asked Bonny, apparently drawn into the concept. "It seems to me that–"

"Are you crazy Bonny?" asked Easy. "Perfection exists. Have you seen the small waist and massive tail on Thelma from 'Good Times'? Now that's perfection...that's perfection!"

Easy's shakes his head with joy at the visualization.

"Ughmm. That's a good idea," stammered Kemet, "but that definition lacks universal application for it is based on opinion, and opinion cannot be the basis for a theory. I therefore prefer to avoid the intrinsic weakness of opinions by establishing a definition that is irrefutable, and I believe that I have accomplished said feat by defining 'perfection' as any state that is completely immutable. To understand, you must accept a few premises concerning perfection that

I wish to study and prove but I do not believe that you will find the premises insurmountable. First, let's–"

"Wait a minute. Wait a minute," disturbed Easy again. "I don't understand. Perfection ain't immutable. What does perfection have to do with being quiet? Now, I dated this one mute girl and I thought it was a good thing at first because I had finally found a woman who wasn't bumping her gums all of the time, but after a while I realized that she wasn't perfect either. I mean, even Easy wants a woman to talk every once in a while, you know?"

Holding back his extreme desire to laugh in Easy's face, Kemet addressed his concern politely because he realized that Easy was not the only person who did not fully understand.

"No. No. Mr. Easy," he chuckled. "Immutable means unable to change. Let me explain. We all can agree that 'perfection' is a state that does not need any additions or reductions because it is perfect; therefore, it does not need to be changed, and with my study, what I am setting out to prove is that *truly* perfect entities, in fact, *cannot* change; thus, it is completely immutable."

Everyone stared at him blankly.

Scanning the confused faces of everyone, Kemet knew he was losing his audience.

"Alright, let me try a different approach. Through religion, we have conceptualized a *perfect* God, correct?" he asked rhetorically. "Now, our perfect God is omnipotent, omnipresent, and immutable and God is the epitome of good and does not change. Realizing that there is nothing on earth like God, the best thing we can do is measure things based on their 'closeness' to God — to perfection. Therefore, the more immutable an object, the closer it is to God because God is immutable. Furthermore, the closer it is to God, the closer it is to being 'good,' and the closer it is to being 'good' determines whether it is more progressive than all other alternatives. It's quite simple, logically. Does everyone understand?"

Everyone shook their heads. Unfortunately, they shook them from side to side. This always seemed to happen. Again, one of his elaborate theories for social progress was incomprehensible to others, and he then knew that the money would be awarded to someone else. At that moment, he lost all hope. Being a "thinker" was his only true desire in life and it saddened him to know that he had put forth so much effort in just this one theory and nothing would come of it.

Nothing ever comes of it.

Kemet dragged his feet back to his seat and slumped backwards.

Mrs. White saw the sadness in his eyes and her motherly instinct took over. "Kemet, please, if there is another way for you to explain it, we are all eager to hear it. I am even willing to grant you more time with your presentation if it helps."

"I thank you Mrs. White but it's no use. It's not your fault. People just don't understand me or anything I talk about anyway." Sadly, he gathered his items and walked outside the door, convinced that Easy would be awarded the money.

As the victor, Easy smiled with pure joy and Bonny could have sworn that she saw every tooth in his mouth. But she, like Mrs. White, also felt bad for the saddened intellectual who slowly dragged his frail body out of the house with a stooped head

"Mr. Easy," whispered Bonny, "have a good heart, will you?"

Outside, Kemet slowly stepped off the porch. With his head still hanging forward, he stepped down and contemplated another occupation. *Maybe I should be a lawyer. At least I won't be so poor...probably won't help change the world, but at least I won't be so dang poor.*

"Listen, young buck," a voice shouted from the front door.

It was Easy.

"I want you to have the money. Don't ask me why, but I kinda feel for you. You're a good kid, you know...a real sincere cat. I know you may not approve of me and what I say and do, but please don't be fooled. You talk all smart and stuff, but it ain't about how well you talk, it's not about what degrees you hold, what institution you attended, hell, it ain't even about what grades or test scores you got. It ain't about none of that. A man's level of intelligence is based on his ability to do things he wasn't taught; his ability to make something outta nothing. That's what blacks have been doing for years and that's what I'm trying to do. You see, My Grandpops had a 3rd grade education and somehow owned and managed his own gas station in Kansas City. Now you can tell me all about white people's concept of intelligence and how only smart people go to college and everything, but most kids come out of school, like my assistant Bonny, and can't tie their shoes. But you, you son, are on the right track. Keep trying to make something outta nothing 'cause that's what we've been doing all along. Who do you think created painting, the world's first tools, written language, mathematics, and all that stuff? Huh? It was *us*. Don't look so surprised, and don't take me for a fool. I know a little something. You're doing the right thing, son. Just don't give up."

With a slap on the shoulder, Easy sent Kemet on his way with the $150,000 check, and Kemet began his seven mile hike back to the bus station with a renewed passion for original thought. He was even more determined than before to create an indicator of progress and regress. He also realized that he now had a newfound respect for the man he once thought was just a bumbling fool. He had never seen such an act of selflessness.

As he started back to the house, Easy knew God was smiling down on him for his deed of selflessness. It was a great sign of progress.

"He just may turn out alright after all," God said to the other gods as they all shook their heads in agreement. It was a beautiful day and God made the sun shine with an even more brilliant sparkle.

I hope you know that I'm expecting something bigger and better than that check for this act of selflessness, Easy smiled and prayed in his mind.

Suddenly, as Easy walked back up the stairs, the porch's top step seemed to reach up and grab his foot. Easy fell face-first into the front door.

S   M   A   C   K!

ABOUT THE AUTHOR

Mr. André Byers is currently a doctoral student. He has a Masters from Harvard University and a Bachelor of Arts from the University of Missouri-Columbia. His areas of concentration have been political theory, black politics, and macroeconomics.

He is the founder and chief executive officer of INGENIUS Press.

Printed in the United States
53626LVS00001B/196-213